W9-AJN-438

The Garden Lover's Guide to Houston

Number Thirty-eight:
W. L. Moody Jr. Natural History Series

A&M travel guides

The Garden Lover's Guide *to* Houston

EILEEN HOUSTON

Foreword by William D. Adams

TEXAS A&M UNIVERSITY PRESS

College Station

Library of Congress Cataloging-in-Publication Data

Houston, Eileen.
The garden lover's guide to Houston /
Eileen Houston ; foreword by William D. Adams. — 1st ed.
p. cm. — (W.L. Moody Jr., natural history series ; no. 38)
Includes index.
ISBN-13: 978-1-58544-613-1 (flexbound : alk. paper)
ISBN-10: 1-58544-613-0 (flexbound : alk. paper)
1. Gardens—Texas—Houston—Guidebooks.
2. Houston (Tex.)—Guidebooks. I. Title.
SB466.U65H684 2007
635.09764'141—dc22
2007003209

This is for my mother, Mary Beere, who was entertained by all the letters I sent home from college—except the ones asking for money. You always said I had a book in me, so here it is. This is for you, Mom, and for Mark, Michele, and Juliet.

Contents

Foreword

Gardeners are constantly searching for new plants or visiting gardens to bring home ideas to incorporate into their own planting designs. Even garden lovers who do not have much time for gardening but appreciate the efforts of others will find this reference a valuable guide to garden exploration in the Houston area. It's a map in easy-to-read text that will help you find the best nurseries, architectural and garden art sources, public gardens, farmer's markets, pick-your-own farms, plant societies, and even a few eateries. Dig (sorry, I couldn't resist) into this manual, and you should quickly come up to speed with garden happenings in and around Houston.

Eileen Houston has done the footwork and uncovered these horticultural gems; fortunately for us, she took good notes. She has written eloquently about them, distilling a few high points from each. If this book doesn't make you want to hit the road to explore gardening opportunities in greater Houston, then you must be passionate about other hobbies. When you get home, you'll have just as much fun planting and displaying your new treasures as you did in discovering them.

—William D. Adams
Harris County Extension Horticulturist Emeritus

Preface

One of my first memories as a child was going out into the lush English cottage garden my mother had planted. Hiding under the lacy white sprays of mock orange, I picked apart bleeding heart flowers and sang to the fairies I knew were hiding nearby. Another memory, one I would like to forget, was the consternation in my mom's voice when I presented her with a fistful of dogwood blossoms I'd swiped from a neighbor's tree. Convinced I'd be jailed, I avoided the friendly neighborhood policeman, who certainly was not my friend.

Better gardening experiences also come to mind: strolling and sampling the ripest fruit from my dad's tomato patch while he imparted his gardening wisdom, along with his fabulous recipe for spaghetti and meatballs. Every time I went back to my childhood home, I could count on a welcoming bouquet that my mom had tucked in the room where I slept.

While living in London, I was fortunate to be able to visit some of the outstanding gardens in Europe, but I marveled at the exquisite little gardens that city dwellers had created on the tiniest patches of ground. I have always had gardens, but it seems that many of my plants went to Vegetation Valhalla due to my overzealous care—or lack thereof.

Deciding to remedy this, I took a Master Gardener course. The first revelation was that even Master Gardeners could occasionally kill plants. I did acquire a great deal of useable information and enjoyed being around other gardeners, who are the sunniest, most cheerful group of people on earth.

I also realized that there were innumerable gardening activities and places clamoring for my time or money, but I didn't know very much about them or where they were located. Reasoning that there were probably many other gardeners, both long-time residents of, and newcomers to, Houston in the same situation, I decided to take action. Thus, this book came about.

Sometimes it is so easy to stay in our own part of town that we become complacent and don't know half of what's out there. While researching this book, I was pleased to discover many delightful locations and activities, and I also met many wonderful people in my forays all over the Houston area.

Keep this book handy. Refer to it often. Read it for entertainment and enlightenment. Whether you're looking for a special plant or a nature-related activity for your children—and there are many of these—get out into the sunshine and have fun!

Acknowledgments

Writing a gardening book is similar to nurturing a favorite fruit tree. You pick the best tree, plant it carefully, give it ample amounts of water and fertilizer, and hope the bugs will pass it by. If all goes well, the tree thrives, blooms, and in time bears fruit for all to enjoy. The analogy ends there. One person can harvest a bushel of fruit from a tree, but a book is a product of the efforts of many, without which it could never come to fruition.

I am grateful beyond words to everyone who helped bring *The Garden Lover's Guide to Houston* into being. Researching it was enjoyable as well as educational. When I visited each destination, many helpful folks were eager to share their knowledge and time. Their enthusiasm is heartwarming, and I learned a great deal from each of them. They reaffirmed my belief that gardeners are the friendliest people on the planet.

All the notes in the world will not morph into a book without a guiding hand or two. Bill Adams, noted author and photographer, was kind enough to review the manuscript and give some valuable advice for polishing it. A very big thank you goes to the staff at Texas A&M University Press, who actually made *The Garden Lover's Guide to Houston* a reality. A huge accolade goes to Shannon Davies, Natural Environment Editor at the Press. She is unfailingly cheerful, supportive, and right on target with her suggestions. My project editor, Jennifer Ann Hobson, and my copy editor, Carol Hoke, both helped me safely navigate the shoals of editing; I am thankful for their guidance.

In addition, family and friends have cheered me on at every step of this journey, never doubting, always encouraging. My husband, Mark, has been my live-in tech support, routinely intoning "Back it up" like a mantra. A true Renaissance man, he also puts together a mouth-watering goat cheese pizza that kept me going. The gardener and her guide thank you, Mark.

xiii

The Garden Lover's Guide to Houston

Cupid and pink hydrangeas—a valentine from Bayou Bend.

Diana the hunter amid the azaleas at Bayou Bend in the springtime.

Exquisite still lifes await you on the Azalea Trail at Bayou Bend.

A floral path at the Azalea Trail at Bayou Bend.

Arching sprays of water frame Diana the hunter at Bayou Bend.

A bird's-eye view of silvery green-and-white foliage in the white garden at Bayou Bend.

Herbs spill over a raised brick bed under a pergola at Houston Garden Center in Hermann Park.

Large boulders, flowing moonrock, and whispering bamboo symbolize the ocean at the entrance to the Japanese Garden.

Carved from a single piece of granite, this lantern houses the spirit of the Japanese Garden.

Blue morpho butterflies snacking on fruit at the Cockrell Butterfly Center.

Winding path of springtime color at Mercer Arboretum.

Classical façade of the River Oaks Garden Club.

Herbs and veggies at the Bayou City Farmers' Market.

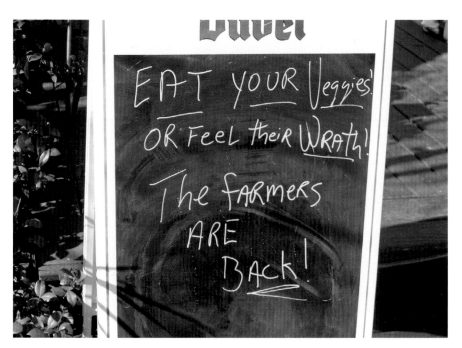

Gentle reminder from the farmers at the Houston Farmers' Market.

Every dog's dream: chewing on delivery people—in the form of a cookie available at the Market Street Farmers' Market.

Orchids for sale at the Market Street Farmers' Market.

Introduction

You have just moved to Houston from Atlanta, Cleveland, or Baltimore and do not know where to find the native plants you have been hearing about. Perhaps you have out-of-town visitors coming in March, and you've heard about the Azalea Trail but are not too sure of the details. You have decided that a cooling splash of water would help the summer sizzle outside—but where can you buy a fountain? Maybe you have a pint-sized crocodile hunter in the family and would prefer to see reptiles in their habitat, not in your bathtub.

This book will answer all of these questions and more. *The Garden Lover's Guide to Houston* is divided into chapters that make it simple to quickly find the information you need. The chapters cover public gardens to visit, garden-related family activities, annual garden events, farms and markets showcasing just-picked produce, garden clubs and societies for every interest, retail sources, book suggestions for your library, volunteer opportunities for gardeners, some great gardening websites, and ideas for day trips outside Houston with a garden theme. For more gardening tidbits, visit my website, www.houstongardenlover.com, which also includes information about travel, food, and wine.

1

The chapters list destinations in alphabetical order, except for the annual garden events, which are listed as they occur during the year. Convenient information about each garden, event, and retail location is at your fingertips, with a map location and website, if one is available. Each resource covers about one page and has an instant summary right above the contact information.

Useful garden-related tips are scattered throughout, and the "Best of the Best" section includes my picks for exceptional locations or events. The choices were difficult, as there are so many little gems out there. Your preferences might differ, but this will get you started on your own road to discovery.

The Garden Lover's Guide to Houston offers a lot of information, but you will find you'll use this book constantly. Keep it in your car, or toss it into a tote bag when you go out. Remember to call ahead before you visit a destination in case the hours of operation have changed.

Thanks to our benign climate, many gardeners call Houston home; a weekend visit to a nursery confirms this. Baby boomers are leading the way, giving up skiing for pursuits kinder to the body, but anyone can find peace in a garden. Here in Houston, we are fortunate to have so many lavish gardens to visit, as well as a huge variety of retail sources. In addition, garden clubs, Master Gardener Associations in each county, and knowledgeable media specialists have a wealth of information and advice when you need it. Don't forget your local nursery—the folks there know what plants grow well in Houston, so you can have a flourishing garden full of greenery that thrives with minimal care.

I wish there had been a book like this when I moved from England to Houston several years ago. It would have saved me a lot of time and money while introducing me to the hidden and not-so-hidden treasures that abound in Houston. Enjoy using *The Garden Lover's Guide to Houston,* and happy exploring!

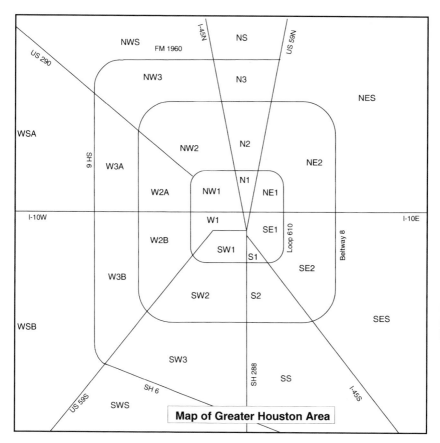

Map of Greater Houston Area

Best of the Best

Here are some of the destinations, gardens, and events that are cherished traditions, unique retail spots, or gardens that will make your heart sing and inspire you. You'll be glad you visited them.

Antique Rose Emporium
Armand Bayou Nature Center
Azalea Trail
Bayou Bend Collection and Gardens
Bayou City Farmers' Market
Bluebonnet Trail
Brookwood Community

Bulb and Plant Mart
Cactus King
Cockrell Butterfly Center
Enchanted Forest Garden Center
McAshan Herb Gardens at Festival Hill
Frazier's Ornamental and Architectural Concrete
Houston Arboretum and Nature Center
Japanese Garden in Hermann Park
Jerry's Jungle Gardens
Joshua's Native Plants and Garden Antiques
Mercer Arboretum and Botanic Gardens
Martha's Bloomers
Moody Gardens
Peckerwood Garden
Poinsettia Celebration at Ellison's Greenhouses
The Arbor Gate
Wabash Antiques and Feed Store
Yucca Do

Gardens Open to the Public

The reasons that people visit public gardens are as varied as the visitors themselves. Some simply want to stroll through beautifully landscaped surroundings, breathing in the fresh lemon-custard scent of a magnolia or letting their eyes feast on the Technicolor fuchsia of a frothy bank of azaleas. Others have a method to their madness, stalking around purposefully and making note of what might enhance their own gardens at home. Some visitors are taking a break from the stresses of daily life in a bustling, noisy city. And some may live in a sophisticated high-rise but crave the sight of a little greenery occasionally.

Any of these large gardens is guaranteed to lift your spirits, perhaps show you how other cultures design their garden spaces, and be a thoroughly delightful place to spend a few hours.

The Bayou Bend gardens are well known since many people visit them on the annual Azalea Trail. Mercer Arboretum's March Mart plant sale introduces plant buyers to the glories of the arboretum. Yet how many Houstonians are aware of the two stellar gardens we have right in town at Hermann Park? More than twenty-five hundred rose plants of many hues and types nestle in their beds in the Houston Garden Center, making it easy to visualize them in your

5

own garden. An island of tranquility in the middle of a noisy city, the Japanese Garden will soothe the harried soul.

Outside the city are several gardens, each with distinctive offerings for the visitor. These are described in the day trip chapter.

Thus, even if you live in a small apartment, you can pretend to be the lord or lady of the manor and stroll through acres of manicured parks or gardens. These grounds are not only beautifully planned and maintained, but they also serve as valuable teaching resources to help you plan your own plots of greenery.

Bayou Bend Collection and Gardens

Elegant, beautiful gardens—the best of the classical style in Texas

Address: One Westcott Street, Houston TX 77007
Phone: 713-639-7750
Website: www.mfah.org
Hours of operation: Tuesday–Saturday 10:00 A.M.–5:00 P.M., Sunday 1:00 P.M.–5:00 P.M., closed Monday (last admission 4:30 P.M.) and major holidays
Admission to gardens $3.00
Directions: East on Memorial Drive inside the Loop. Turn right at Westcott.
Map Location: W1

If you are new to Houston or even if you aren't, this is the place to be in early March. The Azalea Trail takes place then, and Bayou Bend has some of the most breathtaking specimens of this much-loved flowering shrub. In other seasons, there are camellias, magnolias, and crape myrtles to please the eye.

An attractive little footbridge takes you across the bayou to the gardens. Children are fascinated by the topiary garden, which features animals native to Texas grouped around the Lone Star. All ages will enjoy wandering the paths through the wooded ravines.

Daughter of one of the governors of Texas and a leading philanthropist of Houston—she was a founder and president of the Houston Symphony Society—Ima Hogg, who lived here for years, was also an enthusiastic gardener. She supervised the creation of theme gardens here, such as the White Garden, where the heady scents of gardenias, tulips, mock orange, and other white flowers perfume the air, and the Butterfly Garden, so attractive to children, who love to jump on the brickwork forming the butterfly's body while enjoying the colorful azaleas that constitute the wings. Miss Hogg's sense of humor resulted in the creation of the Carla Garden, in commemoration of the hurricane of 1961, which caused so much devastation to her gardens.

A charming trio of gardens is dedicated to three of the Greek muses of the arts. Clio, the muse of history, presides over a curved, geometric garden laden with roses and other perennials. In the garden opposite rests Euterpe, the muse of music, a subject dear to the heart of Miss Hogg, who was an accomplished pianist. An informal arrangement of azaleas, redbuds, and magnolias ensures blooms year-round in the Euterpe Garden.

The highlight of the three gardens is the Diana Garden, dedicated to the goddess of the hunt. From the porch of Bayou Bend, a breathtaking view unfolds. Yaupon hedges frame the walls of the outdoor room and draw your gaze down the length of the garden to the snow-white statue of the huntress. Graceful arching streams of water further focus your eye on Diana, while formally pruned yews behind her accentuate her even more.

As dazzling as the gardens are, do not forget about the beauties of the home itself. Bayou Bend was built in 1927 by Miss Hogg and her brothers, and she lived there until 1966, when she generously presented the house and its collections to the Museum of Fine Arts in Houston. For devotees of world-class American colonial furnishings, Bayou Bend's collections are unsurpassed. Some of the best-known American craftspersons and artists, such as Paul Revere, Charles Willson Peale, and John Singleton Copley, are represented.

7

Houston Garden Center in Hermann Park

Got roses? Get great ideas here for keeping them happy.

Address: 1500 Hermann Drive, Houston TX 77004
Phone: 713-284-1989
Website: www.houstontx.gov/parks/hermannpark.html
Hours of operation: Monday–Friday 8:00 A.M.–6:00 P.M.; weekends and holidays 10:00 A.M.– 6:00 P.M.
Directions: in Hermann Park, which is near the Texas Medical Center
Map Location: SW1

This is a wonderful place to learn about many plants, especially roses and herbs, both of which have extensive gardens devoted to them. Be aware, though, that there is no gift shop or library here, just gardens. The stately building you see is a meeting place for many of the plant societies around our town.

On a hot day, it's a kind of aromatherapy to breathe in the heady scent wafting from the beds and beds of roses. Birds trill as you walk on the pathways between the roses, which are lovingly pampered in raised beds. You might see a rose that attracts you with its scent, growth habit, or profusion of blooms. Lo and behold, there's a tag identifying it, so you do not have to guess what rose it might be. Roses are a little particular about where they want to be planted, so it is worth your while to pay attention to how the folks here have done it.

Several other gardens can provide ideas for your own garden projects. A perennial garden is helpful for newcomers to the area to see what plants come back year after year. Bright yellow rudbeckias, fuchsia pentas, graceful pink echinaceas, and other plants loved by butterflies, bees, and hummingbirds flourish here. Children will want to touch the "cat's whiskers" perennial, with its soft spiky fronds. Persimmon trees do well in Houston, and the orangey-red fruits are a welcome bonus. For a damp spot in the landscape, gather inspiration from the bog garden.

As you wander through the various gardens, you will see several statues dedicated to former leaders of Central and South American countries.

The herb garden was developed in 1961 and 1962 by Madalene Hill, a well-known herb expert, who devised the plant list for it. Grown in large raised brick beds, the preferred setting for herbs in our area, they flourish under the beams of a semishaded wooden pergola. Each bed has a theme: rosemary bed, culinary bed, lemon bed, potpourri bed, knot garden, and scented geranium bed. Stop and rest on a bench under the dappled light of the pergola, breathe in the exotic perfumes of the various herbs, take a deep breath, and enjoy. Favorites might be the lemon bed, which has all of the citrusy lemon-scented herbs, or the rosemary bed, full of the many cultivars of this fragrant, pine-scented culinary plant. Again, everything is labeled, so you can take notes for your own herb plot.

Lynn R. Lowrey Arboretum at Rice University

The wealth of native plants adorning the campus at Rice is a fitting tribute to Lynn Lowrey.

Address: Rice University campus, bounded by Rice Boulevard, Main Street, University Boulevard, and Greenbriar, Houston TX 77004
Phone: 713-348-5736
Website: www.arboretum.rice.edu
Hours of operation: daily during daylight hours
Directions: From downtown, drive south along Main Street to University Boulevard, turn right, then turn right again at Greenbriar. Enter the free parking area from Greenbriar. Rice University is near the Texas Medical Center and inside Loop 610.
Map Location: SW1

Founder of the native plant movement in Texas, Lynn Lowrey earned that title because of his enthusiasm for these natives that grew so well here. He was a tireless advocate, giving away "pass along" plants to anyone who would accept them, trying to convert people to the concept that these natives were not only fuss free but also attractive in the landscape. It is only fitting that this arboretum bears his name.

The acknowledged beauty of the Rice campus pays homage to

Gardens Open to the Public

the diversity of trees and greenery from the Texas and northern Mexico areas. At least twelve varieties of oak trees can be found, lending a graceful dignity and providing shade and softness to the buildings. Other woody plants you might see as you walk around campus include hickories, maples, and hollies. One historical specimen of note is the Pershing tree, a robust, attractive pecan tree planted in 1920 by Gen. John J. Pershing, the World War I commander of the Allied Expeditionary Forces. This tree sits in splendor on Founder's Court, an open, grassy area bordered with oaks and magnolias that is located toward the eastern end of campus.

To the east of the soccer stadium lies the Harris Gully Natural Area. For those whose eyes are used to viewing a manicured garden, this area might look a bit wild and wooly. But that's exactly the point; it *is* wild—and demonstrates how central Houston looked before civilization arrived. Oaks hung with trailing gray scarves of Spanish moss share space with numerous varieties of grasses, as well as familiar and lesser-known garden favorites like black-eyed Susans, verbenas, mallows, bundleflower, frogbit, and alligator weed. The names of these long-used native plants reads like a history of the pioneers that first grew them, studied their habits, and gave them names that we still use today.

The Botany Garden, located between the geology and biology buildings, is a work in progress. Currently, five greenhouses are under construction. These will house unusual plants available for study by botany students. An eye-catching demonstration garden already started will show off many of these native specimens, such as dry bed and habitat plantings. Golden black-eyed Susans pair well with the fuzzy purple-and-white flowering wands of Mexican bush sage and red-flowered firebush.

Peaceful spots to enjoy the garden beauty are dotted around campus; rest by a trickling fountain and pond at the Commons Courtyard or on the shady patio behind Rice Memorial Center. Look around and be grateful that Lynn Lowrey cared so much about the native plants of our state.

Mercer Arboretum and Botanic Gardens

This is a treasure for all of us, at all seasons.

Address: 22306 Aldine Westfield Road, Humble TX 77338

Phone: 281-443-8731

Website: www.hcp4.net/mercer

Hours of operation: Monday–Saturday 8:00 A.M.–7:00 P.M., Sunday 10:00
A.M.–7:00 P.M. in summer; daily 8:00 A.M.–5:00 P.M. in winter

Directions: I-45 north to FM 1960, turn east. Turn left at Aldine Westfield
Road, then go 1¼ miles and turn left at the light into the arboretum, or go
right for the visitor center.

Map Location: NS

No matter what season of the year you visit Mercer Arboretum, the gardens are always spectacular. Named after Thelma and Charles Mercer, who purchased the original 14 acres in the 1940s and built their home there, Mercer Arboretum now covers more than 250 acres. The Mercers were careful to preserve the many large trees already growing there, adding several unusual species and planting large camellias. The property is divided into two areas along Aldine Westfield Road: The Botanic Gardens are on the east side, and the Arboretum is on the west side.

The gardens engage all five of your senses. Everywhere you gaze, beautiful plant combinations please the eye. The soft smell of pine needles and aromatic herbs, warmed by the sun, perfumes the air. With all the choice habitat available, birds live happily here and fill the woods with their trills. Little breezes touch your skin and cool you. And the sense of taste? Though it is not a good idea to taste any of the plants, there is a picnic area and barbecue pavilion where you can tame your hunger.

An eye-catching fountain with water lilies, bog plants, and bronze adornments lies adjacent to the visitor center of the botanic gardens on the east side of Mercer. Nearby, the herb garden displays all kinds of culinary and medicinal herbs, as well as some grown for their literary associations. Shakespeare wrote of many herbs, such as rosemary and rue, in his plays. If you love gingers, do not miss

11

Gardens Open to
the Public

the ginger garden with its 150 species, one of the largest collections in the country.

Other gardens also beckon. Mercer Botanic Garden is a wonderful inspiration for those of you who are new to gardening and need a little imaginative push. Specially planned areas are devoted to color plants, salvias, perennials, vines, rock plantings, daylilies, shady bogs, tropical plants, ferns, bamboo, and azaleas. The naturalist will enjoy the prehistoric plant and endangered species gardens. Farther along, a teahouse nestles near a lush lily pond, strewn lavishly with a huge collection of Louisiana irises.

To the west lies the arboretum, with its collections of woodland plants and trees. This is the place for family hikes, where everyone can enjoy the peace, birdsong, fresh air, and perhaps a picnic or barbecue at a table in a shaded setting.

A highlight of Mercer Arboretum is an outstanding educational program covering a wide range of topics taught by experts in various fields. Enthusiastic volunteers help keep these gardens shipshape for all to enjoy and assist with the annual March Mart plant sale.

The Japanese Garden in Hermann Park

A gracious gift from the people of Japan to the people of Houston

Address: Hermann Park, Houston TX 77030
Phone: 713-284-1914
Website: www.houstontx.gov/parks/hermannpark.html
Hours of operation: Daily 10:00 A.M.–6:00 P.M. in spring and summer; daily 10:00 A.M.–5:00 P.M. in fall and winter
Directions: West side of Hermann Park, which is near the Texas Medical Center
Map Location: SW1

The
Garden Lover's
Guide to
Houston

It is hard to imagine a busier place in our city than the Texas Medical Center. Yet nearby in Hermann Park is a secret oasis of calm and beauty: the Japanese Garden. Designed by noted Japanese landscape artist Ken Nakajima, this serene spot was a collaboration between businesses both here and in Japan. It is designed as a *daimyo* garden, a recreational one, as opposed to the perhaps more familiar Zen garden, which is usually found near temples.

For centuries, Japanese gardens have been carefully composed with great regard for symbolism. The dry landscape garden at the entrance represents a seascape: Large boulders indicate landmasses, the black moon rock is the sea, and the swishing of the bamboo conjures up the sound of the ocean. Houston's sister city, Chiba, Japan, gave us the granite welcoming lantern, in which the spirit of the garden is said to repose.

You observe that all of the paths are curved and run from east to west. Curved paths not only change the viewpoint constantly as you stroll along but also keep evil from following you, according to Buddhist belief.

The trickling of water from a small stream serenades as you wend your way from one tranquil vista to another. Picturesque bridges crisscross the stream, and graceful aquatic plants furnish hiding places and food for the darting koi. Ducks waddle by, but please resist the urge to feed them, the squirrels, or the fish.

A focal point of the garden is the teahouse, the *azumaya*. Built in Japan of Hinoki cypress and other traditional materials, it has mortise-and-tenon construction for the joints; no nails were used. The centuries-old Japanese tea ceremony is presented here.

Cherry trees in bloom are one of the sights most beloved by the Japanese. Evoking their blossoms, crepe myrtles in many shades of pink add their lacy and refreshing charm to this springlike vista. A waterfall tumbles over huge boulders of Texas pink granite into the still pond below.

A wealth of textural and color variety ensures beautiful blooms and foliage at any time of the year. You will be calmed, uplifted, and refreshed by a stroll through this serene garden.

13

For Children of All Ages

What a wealth of children's outdoor activities Houston offers! In this chapter you may be able to find an answer for that end-of-summer whine, "I'm bored." When your nieces and nephews are in town, pack everyone into the van and head for one of these spots. Everyone is guaranteed to have fun while learning about the flora and fauna around them. Who knows—you might inspire a future National Geographic explorer.

When the children need to work off some steam, take off for one of these areas for hiking, biking, observing wildlife, or bird watching. After the kids are tired out, they can view the exhibits and participate in the activities geared toward different age groups.

Your children might visit some of these parks or centers on a school trip; if not, be sure that you take them yourself. If you have Girl or Boy Scouts in the family, they can often earn badges in conjunction with work or study at these locations. For the littlest preschoolers, the attractions include fuzzy animal puppets to play with, singing, and story hours. And the resources for science projects are tremendous.

Many if not most of these venues have weeklong summer day camp programs, as well as weekend programs during the school year. Some even have minicamps that take place during school breaks. The prices are reasonable when you consider what fun the kids have and how much they benefit.

Volunteers are the golden heart of these programs; their untiring help and enthusiasm for the children they introduce to nature's wonders are heartwarming. So put on your hiking shoes or tennies, hop in the car, and prepare for great adventures. Each of these locations has its own unique charms, and each awaits your discovery.

Cockrell Butterfly Center

A magnificent home for these living jewels

Address: 1 Hermann Circle Drive, Houston 77030
Phone: 713-639-4629
Website: www.hmns.org
Hours of operation: Monday–Saturday 9:00 A.M.–5:00 P.M., Sunday 11:00 A.M.–5:00 P.M.
Admission fee: adults, $8; children age 3–11, $6; under 3, free
Directions: In the Houston Museum of Natural Science (HMNS) in Hermann Park, at the intersection of Caroline and Hermann streets, across from the Miller Outdoor Theater
Map Location: SW1

If you do not know a butterfly from a moth, don't worry—the friendly folks here will direct you to a small theater where you can view a short film that orients you to everything the Cockrell Butterfly Center has to offer. There is also a handy laminated identification chart to help you identify the Monarch butterfly that alights on a flower as you walk by. This is a wonderful place for children to see the interrelationship between people and the environment.

Butterflies are shipped here from Central America in chrysalis form, glued to string and boards. They do not move or eat and are displayed on the wall for you to study. Eventually they will mature into the familiar butterfly forms we all recognize. You then enter the 70-by-100-foot greenhouse habitat, built to mimic a Central Amer-

The
Garden Lover's
Guide to
Houston

ican rainforest. On the main level is a waterfall, just as you would find in the rainforest, with bird and animal calls recorded in Costa Rica adding to the ambiance.

Then look up—the soaring, sunlit space is in motion with delicate, jewel-toned butterflies flitting between the flowers or resting and dining on fruit nectars at feeders. Look down, and if you're lucky, you might catch sight of Sidney, the male iguana, colorful with his blue jowls and orange dewlaps. Have no fear; he's very tame.

Close up, you might see a rice paper butterfly sipping nectar from a magenta penta flower. Take pictures of the colorful parrots that inhabit the "forest." Benches are placed at intervals so that you can sit and enjoy the surroundings. When you leave the hall, please check for "hitchhikers" on your clothes: A butterfly might mistake your floral dress for the real thing and hop a ride into the great outdoors.

In summer, children attending camp at the museum fill the halls, dashing to and fro, looking like brightly colored butterflies themselves in their camp T-shirts. Volunteers are very knowledgeable and friendly to everyone. Of course, you can also pick up tips for creating a butterfly-friendly garden of your own.

The entomology department can answer all of the bug questions the kids have, and parents will enjoy the HMNS gift shops. If you're hungry, fast food is available. There is even more to see in the rest of the museum, so allow some time to take in the other exhibits as well.

Edith L. Moore Nature Sanctuary

If it has feathers, here's the place to learn about it.

Address: 440 Wilchester Boulevard, Houston TX 77079

Phone: 713-932-1639

Website: www.houstonaudubon.org

Hours of operation: October–March 7:00 A.M.–7:00 P.M., April–September
    7:00 A.M.–9:00 P.M.

Directions: West on Memorial Drive from the Sam Houston Tollway. Go left
    at the light for Wilchester Boulevard, then south for a few blocks.

Map Location: W2B

For Children of
All Ages

If, when August comes, you fill the hummingbird feeders to attract these tiny speed demons and if you gnash your teeth at every sunflower seed lost to voracious squirrels, then you are probably a birder. And if you haven't been to the Edith L. Moore Bird Sanctuary, hidden in the pines of Memorial, then you're missing a treat. Not only are there birds to see as you hike the trails, but this is also the headquarters of the Houston Audubon Society, and that means many fascinating and informative programs.

In 1932 Edith L. Moore and her husband built a log cabin here as a getaway from the bustling city that was Houston, cutting the pine logs from their own land. At that time, dairy farming and logging were the main activities in Memorial, not mall crawling and softball. The Moores donated the cabin and the seventeen surrounding acres to the city in 1975, and the site became a focus for birding activities and education.

The well-maintained hiking trails are dotted with benches to entice you to stop and listen to the liquid "what cheer" sound of a cardinal, breathe the pine-scented air, or just commune with nature and revel in the quiet. Four-legged hikers may come, too, but they must be leashed, and visitors are asked to stay on the trails with them.

At the nature sanctuary you and your children can not only see the birds but learn about them, too. Preschoolers will enjoy the Titmouse Club, where the little ones can go on a nature walk, listen to stories, and participate in a variety of activities. The enthusiastic docents preside over birthday parties where the children have fun creating nature-themed crafts. The docents also direct camp activities, including Nature Explorer Day Camp, guided tours, Camp Tadpole in summer, Pond Camp, and Owl Prowls at night. The Houston Audubon Society has plenty of other activities ranging from bird counts to lectures to field trips, so that even the most energetic child or adult will find plenty to do.

Houston Arboretum and Nature Center

Talk with the animals; walk with the animals; grunt, squeak, and squawk with the animals.

Address: 4501 Woodway, Houston TX 77024

Phone: 713-681-8433

Website: www.houstonarboretum.org

Hours of operation: 8:30 A.M.–6:00 P.M. daily. The building, which houses the Discovery Room, Nature Shop, library, classrooms, and offices, is open daily from 9:00 A.M. to 5:00 P.M. The Discovery Room hours are 10:00 A.M.–4:00 P.M. daily, closed on Mondays. The Nature Shop is open 10:00 A.M.–4:00 P.M. daily.

Directions: Take Loop 610 west, go north to Woodway, and exit to the east on Woodway. Soon after you get on Woodway, turn right into the arboretum.

Map Location: W1

After dealing with the traffic, noise, and an overscheduled lifestyle every day, do you feel frazzled? Then head for this inner-loop green oasis of peace where you can unwind and recharge your batteries. This is a not-to-be-missed spot, whatever your nature interests may be. While parents can enjoy watching the birds, identifying trees and shrubs, or just meandering down a quiet path, this place seems to have been created for children, who find plenty to attract them.

First, the Discovery Room will teach them about the three habitats at the arboretum, but in a way that makes learning fun. Children can peer at tiny insects under a microscope, get involved with interactive media, and learn from the many exhibits. Even the littlest toddlers will love cuddling the plush animals and birds in this room.

And if this is not enough for your pint-sized Doctor Doolittles, they can have even more fun at the naturalist explorer classes, which have intriguing titles such as "Extreme Mice and Rats" and "Webslingers." The littlest children can be Tadpole Troopers, listening to stories, playing games, and making crafts, while accompanied by an adult.

Summer camp classes involving both indoor and outdoor activities teach children about topics such as weird weather and the magic

19

For Children of
All Ages

of flight. Registration for the summer camps begins in March. Girl and Boy Scouts can earn badges through the programs here, and adults can even become certified naturalists.

The arboretum and nature center offer something for everyone, including a well-stocked nature-themed shop with squiggly worms and other creepy crawlies for the children and gifts for the adults. If you want to learn more about the critters you see, browse a bit in the well-stocked library.

Picnicking is not allowed at the arboretum, but the nearby Memorial Park provides picnic facilities, and you can also bike, walk the dog, or play golf. So make an afternoon of it and come home rejuvenated, ready for the rat race, and maybe knowing more about the rats, too.

Jesse H. Jones Park and Nature Center

Up close and personal with Mother Nature

Address: 20634 Kenswick Drive, Humble TX 77338
Phone: 281-446-8588
Website: www.hcp4.net/jones
Hours of operation: December and January 8:00 A.M.–5:00 P.M.; November and February 8:00 A.M.–6:00 P.M.; March to October 8:00 A.M.–7:00 P.M.
Directions: Take I-45 north to FM 1960, then go east to Kenswick Drive, and then north to the park entrance.
Map Location: NS

As you approach the nature center building, you will notice the native wildflowers blooming in front. Signs posted on the fence depict animal tracks of critters you would expect to see, such as possum, deer, armadillo, and turkey—but wolf and bear? Don't worry; you won't have to look over your shoulder for these last two.

Learn about the flora and fauna in the park from the informative displays of live reptiles and snakes, as well as the stuffed possums, beavers, and other animals. Children are fascinated by the comings and goings of the honeybees, whose hive opens to the outdoors. Above, mounted birds of prey "soar" as if they were in flight.

Now it's time to go outdoors and see the park itself. Located on Spring Creek, Jones Park consists of 225 acres of diverse habitat, including white sand beaches, cypress bogs, and wildflower meadows. There's plenty to occupy the kids here: hiking along more than five miles of paved trails, fishing, climbing around a large playground with nearby barbecue facilities, even canoeing on guided trips. Or how about a lazy afternoon spent on a guided pontoon boat tour of Spring Creek?

Visit a re-creation of a pioneer Texas log cabin, the Redbud Hill Homestead, and see what life was like before Nintendo and fast food. Other outbuildings include the barn, the smokehouse, and woodworking and blacksmithing buildings, where you can watch demonstrations of these activities. A re-creation of an Akokisa Indian village includes the council lodge and chief's hut. Introduce your littlest angler to fishing on the banks of Spring Creek—a great photo op and memory maker.

The entertainment doesn't end yet. Saturday and Sunday programs with intriguing titles such as "Plants with Attitude," "Tree T's," and "Peel and Squeal" help kids and their parents learn about wildflowers, carnivorous plants, butterflies, animal tracks, pioneer life, and so on. A summer nature day camp is great fun for youngsters ages 5–12, and the Tadpoles Club is designed for kids 3–4 years of age.

With its celebration of Pioneer Day in November and Texas Heritage Day in the spring, Jones Park keeps our Texas heritage alive for future generations. In addition, Scouts can earn badges through programs at the park. The schedule each month is absolutely crammed with activities for all ages, and, best of all, much of it is free.

Nature Discovery Center

The name says it all.

Address: 7112 Newcastle, Houston TX 77401
Phone: 713-667-6550
Website: www.naturediscoverycenter.org
Hours of operation: Tuesday–Sunday, noon to 5:30 P.M., closed on Mondays

For Children of
All Ages

Directions: Inside Loop 610 in Bellaire, on Newcastle, between Bellaire Boulevard and Evergreen

Map Location: SW1

Who would have guessed that in the heart of Bellaire you would find the Nature Discovery Center, a spot that lives up to its name; here you'll discover nature in many of its fascinating forms. The center, located in the Henshaw home in Bellaire, houses two Discovery Rooms with hands-on interactive exhibits. Children can watch live snakes, reptiles, a turtle, and a cute guinea pig. Discovery Boxes, modeled after those at the Smithsonian, give a peek at different topics in a way that captures children's interest. Games and puzzles make learning even more fun.

How about a "Creepy Crawlies" birthday party for your 4-to-10-year-olds, where they will learn the truth about animals that scare people, complete with specimens and live animals? Or a "Bunny Buddies" party for 2- to 4-year-olds, starring a cuddly rabbit to pet?

Many classes for kids fill the schedule. Preschoolers can listen to a story at Nature Story time each Wednesday at 1 P.M. Preschoolers can be Nature Detectives, take nature walks, make crafts, learn songs, and play with puppets to introduce them to science. Their school-age companions are the Eco Explorers, who study insects and ecology and will put that chemistry set to good use.

What do you do with your kids when there's a school holiday or teacher workday? A great solution is the "break-out camp," where children have fun while they learn at these one-day camps. Week-long science camps for ages five to ten are held during the summer. During the winter holiday season, children can make gifts for their favorite people at a holiday craft workshop, while you take a break for a few hours.

Piles of orange pumpkins, hayrides in horse-drawn wagons, food, games, craftspeople selling books, yard art, and jewelry—it must be October and therefore time for the annual Pumpkin Patch. Both young and old will love this activity. Moms and dads will also enjoy the annual "Bug Ball," when the park is aglow with lights and glittering butterflies; the event is quite beautiful and not at all buggy, as the name might suggest. Parents can bid on items at the live or silent auctions and then dance the night away.

Robert A. Vines Environmental Science Center

You'll have a new appreciation for our Texas animals and plants.

Address: 8856 Westview Drive, Houston TX 77055
Phone: 713-365-4175
Website: none listed
Hours of operation: Monday–Friday 8:30 A.M.–4:30 P.M.
Directions: I-10 west, exit Bingle, north on Bingle, left on Westview
Map Location: W2A

This is a hidden secret in the Spring Branch area that not everyone knows about unless they have children in the Spring Branch school district who have taken a field trip to this spot. The public can come here too, and they will find a surprisingly well-organized series of halls covering geology, oceanography, exotic animals, natural history, and wildlife sciences. There's an arboretum, too.

Children will like the dioramas showing the different habitats in the Houston area. Life-sized denizens of the swamp, the forest, and other areas are depicted going about their lives. The geology hall boasts a thirty-three-foot dinosaur, the Allosaurus, as well as a T. rex head—what big teeth he had!

To evoke the maritime environment, a life-sized polar bear and two seals greet you as you enter the oceanography hall, which is home to all kinds of fish, including sharks, and marine mammals, such as dolphins (both big and little), as well as seashells.

The Spring Branch botanical garden is at the entrance to the center. The garden, which was donated by Anderson Landscape and Nursery, contains plants native to the southern part of the United States and northern Mexico. They are labeled, which makes it easy to jot down the name of that shrub that would look so good on the patio.

A stroll through the five-acre arboretum will acquaint you with about two hundred varieties of native Texas trees, shrubs, and vines. The walk is a peaceful one, punctuated by the warbling sounds of birds.

For Children of
All Ages

In the aquatic study area, several fish species swim freely in a pond. When you pause on the wooden bridge over the pond, you just might surprise some large frogs or toads, who will respond to your arrival with a loud splash into the water.

For the adults, there are bird-watching classes and spring and fall wildflower seminars. In addition, travel programs have covered destinations such as Venezuela, Trinidad, and the Galapagos Islands.

This fence-sitting tomcat at the Antique Rose Emporium appears startled.

The imposing gate at Antique Rose Emporium marks the entryway to the enchanted gardens within.

Adorable Beatrix Potter bunnies in the children's garden at the Antique Rose Emporium.

A colorful bottle tree at the Antique Rose Emporium.

Rush hour for the feral hogs at Brazos Bend State Park.

A concrete calf begs for attention at Frazier's Concrete.

Concrete canines seem to be ignoring the nearby fire hydrant at Frazier's Concrete.

A row of boots and weathered Lone Stars from Martha's Bloomers are rustic accents for a Texas garden.

A colorful planting at Martha's Bloomers highlights plants unfazed by summer heat.

Old-fashioned hollyhocks frame a view of the Menke House and the herbs at McAshan Herb Gardens.

This view at McAshan Herb Gardens could be mistaken for one in the Mediterranean.

Mellowed stone blocks lend a textural contrast to the burgundy and green coleus and salvias at McAshan Herb Gardens.

Neoclassical introduction to the medicinal herbs in the pharmacy garden at McAshan Herb Gardens.

Rising from the greenery surrounding it, the rainforest pyramid at Moody Gardens resembles its Egyptian namesake.

Two scarlet macaws interrupt their conversation to stare at visitors to Moody Gardens.

Striking textural and color contrasts of yucca and agave demonstrate the beauty of dry climate plantings at Peckerwood Garden.

Simple yet sculptural masks typical of Mexico are among the art objects at Peckerwood Garden.

A taro at Peckerwood Garden appears to be splashed with shades of green, yellow, and white paint by an artist.

Even the cows are decked out for the Poinsettia Celebration at Ellison's.

This rosy pink poinsettia from Ellison's appears to have been dipped in gold.

If old man winter passes you by, these curly white poinsettias from Ellison's can evoke a snow scene.

Magnificent iron welcome sign at Shimek's Gardens highlights the daylilies in May.

Sunny daylilies show off against a deep purple background at Shimek's Gardens.

Food for the butterflies and birds at the Texas A&M holistic gardens.

Gazebo bordered by maroon and white plantings at the Texas A&M holistic gardens.

Relax on the patio while enjoying the raised accessible garden beds at the Texas A&M holistic gardens.

Typical Texas icons welcome you to the Texas A&M horticultural gardens.

A cheerful entry sign to the Texas A&M horticultural gardens.

Giant swallowtail butterflies sip nectar from zinnias at the Texas A&M horticultural gardens.

Annual Garden Events

Houstonians enthusiastically mark the passing of the seasons with many events that celebrate the abundance of green and growing things that we enjoy. Whether it is a plant sale or a trail that pays homage to a particular flower, there is a year-round calendar of happenings to sample.

To a Houston gardener, March means it's time to rev up the pickup and head for Mercer Arboretum's March Mart plant sale, which features many specimens not usually seen in nurseries. Later in the year, October brings cooler weather and the annual Bulb and Plant Mart, where gardeners can plan ahead for a kaleidoscope of springtime blooms. Bulb growers worldwide send their best stock to this sale.

We have many time-honored traditions to mark the change of seasons; these are just a few of the many garden events and sales year-round. Be sure to dress comfortably for the plant sales, and bring a wagon for your finds. Gardeners, usually amiable people, sometimes engage in a buying frenzy, and the early bird does get the rare ginger.

For inspiration and sheer beauty, the Azalea and Bluebonnet Trails, as well as the Poinsettia Celebration, are hard to beat (the for-

25

mer is described later in this chapter, and the latter two are covered in the chapter on day trips). Not only do they offer everyone a chance to appreciate three favorite flowers, but they also keep alive the idea of celebrating traditions, which can sometimes get lost in our hectic lives. All three offer wonderful photo ops, so pack your camera. And don't forget the bottled water.

There are several other sales, trails, and gatherings of gardeners to inspire you. Check your newspaper for other events; something garden-related is happening every week, including lectures, classes, demonstrations, and celebrations.

January, February, April, and September
Harris County Master Gardener Association (HCMGA)
   Plant Sales

February and October
Texas Home and Garden Show

March
Azalea Trail
Mercer Arboretum March Mart

March and April
Bluebonnet Trail (see Day Trips chapter)

October
Bulb and Plant Mart

November
Poinsettia Celebration at Ellison's Greenhouse (see Day
   Trips chapter)
Nutcracker Market

Master Gardener Association Plant Sales

Pampered plants and helpful Master Gardeners, too

Address: 3033 Bear Creek Drive, Houston TX 77084, and other locations
Phone 281-855-5600
Website: http://hcmga.tamu.edu
Dates and times: These vary; check the website or Saturday's *Houston Chronicle*.
Directions: West on I-10 to SH 6, turn right. Go right on Patterson Road, then
   turn left for Extension offices.
Map Location: W3A

What plant could be better than one that has been lovingly grown and tended by someone who knows its every need? The Harris County Master Gardeners sponsor plant sales where you can not only buy attractive or unusual plants that are priced well but also find out how to keep them happy once you get them home. Master Gardener Associations in other counties have sales, too.

The HCMGA sponsors four plant sales a year, usually held in January, February, April, and September, targeted toward the season of the year in which each occurs. Thus, the January sale features fruit trees, as that is the time of year to plant them. You can select all kinds of stone fruit trees, such as peaches for that creamy home-made peach ice cream. If your dreams include picking lemons or oranges from your own trees for tasty tropical fruit concoctions, look no farther. And nothing beats a freshly baked, juicy blueberry pie from a crop you have grown yourself—it's *mouthwatering*.

Get a head start on tomatoes with the tomato and pepper sale in February. Heirloom and other old favorite varieties, plus some newer disease-resistant kinds are available as healthy young plants, ready to go into your tomato patch. And what a variety of peppers— try green, red, or yellow bell peppers or some flaming hot ones that really light your fire.

April brings the spring plant sale, just in time for all the feverish activity taking place in the garden at this time of year. As with all of the sales, the plants are in tip-top condition and include some unusual and hard-to-find specimens. As a bonus, Master Gardeners are available to answer your questions about a plant's care and feeding.

27

Believe it or not, fall is one of the best times for gardening in Houston. The temperature has cooled off a bit, so this is actually a great time to plant perennials. They have a chance to settle in and develop a good root system over the winter. If you want to attract hummingbirds and butterflies to your flower bower, you can find what you need here. Herbs, irises, daylilies, and roses can help fill out the bare spots in your garden.

I cannot say enough good things about all of the wonderful people in the Master Gardener program, which you will read more about in the Volunteer Opportunities chapter.

Texas Home and Garden Show

It's all here, under one roof.

Address: 8400 Kirby Drive, Houston TX 77054 (Reliant Event Center)
Website: www.texashomeandgarden.com
Hours of operation: Friday 2:00 P.M.–9:00 P.M., Saturday 10:00 A.M.–9:00 P.M., Sunday 11:00 A.M.–6:00 P.M. for February show; October show closes at 8:00 P.M. Friday and Saturday.
Directions: Loop 610 west to Kirby Drive; turn right (north) on Kirby. Follow signs to parking. Parking and admission charge; discount admission coupon at website
Map Location: SW1

Can't visualize how to fit a bronze, life-sized Longhorn into the garden? Help is here, with hundreds of displays where exhibitors can help you find the best pools, water features, landscaping, and those little niceties like barbecues and garden art. Redecorate the indoors as well, with state of the art appliances and furnishings. And if you do not already know what fire ants are, you definitely will when you leave.

Rather than wasting your valuable time driving from place to place looking at water features until you feel as though you're drowning, why not see them in one place? The exhibitors are eager to answer your questions and give you literature that you can read at home when the rain is pouring down.

If you want to have an instant showpiece garden while letting someone else do all of the work, landscapers are also present. The latest technology in outdoor grilling is available, too, so that you can have your own outdoor kitchen and barbecue just like the pros.

Once you have spiffed up the garden, it's time to decorate it. Beautifully glazed pottery, sparkling hanging metal sculptures that turn in the breeze, concrete squirrels and rabbits, dreamy gazing balls in jewel-toned colors—the list of sale items goes on and on.

Let's not forget decking the halls: There are numerous ways to make your interior spaces as cozy or dramatic as you wish. Everything from furniture to lamps to artwork is here for the buying.

If you have questions about those critters running around in the garden or the huge caterpillar munching on your coveted tomatoes, the friendly Master Gardener folks will provide suggestions. There's even a fire ant booth to help you keep the little devils away from your happy home. Here you can learn all about the Texas Two-Step, the preferred method for keeping the little nuisances at bay.

Azalea Trail

Celebrate spring with lush gardens full of colorful azaleas.

Address: Bayou Bend, 1 Westcott Street, Houston TX 77007, Rienzi, and
　　other private homes in the River Oaks area
Phone: 713-523-2483
Website: www.riveroaksgardenclub.org
Hours of operation: Friday–Sunday 11:00 A.M.–6:00 P.M. for one weekend in
　　early March
Admission: Seven admissions are $15.00 in advance sales at local plant shops
　　and nurseries; on the days of the Azalea Trail, seven admissions are $20.00,
　　and single tickets are $5.00. Children 12 and under are admitted free.
Directions: See Bayou Bend listing for Bayou Bend Gardens.
Map Location: W1

Is there a more glorious way to celebrate spring than to tour some of Houston's most dazzling gardens billowing with multihued azaleas? Sponsored by the River Oaks Garden Club, this well-attended event features several stops at some of our city's finest gardens. Shades of pink, fuchsia, purple, white, and even red and yellow are a feast for the eyes. To winter-weary visitors from up north, this is paradise—and not to be missed.

The best place to begin is at the Bayou Bend Gardens, a fourteen-acre showcase for this gorgeous spring bloomer. The property is divided into separate gardens, each with its own unique character. Walk though the dappled forested areas of the Woodland Trails garden to see azaleas in a wilder setting interspersed with the lacy flower-filled branches of dogwood, and then enjoy the more formal displays nearer to the mansion. Formed from three shades of azaleas, the pink wings on the large butterfly in the Butterfly Garden will entrance children.

You could also start your tour at the River Oaks Garden Club Forum, the club's headquarters. Here you will find local experts to answer your azalea questions and members who will demonstrate how to arrange these and other flowers. This is a good place to pick up horticultural information. The club has published a good guide for Houston gardeners, *A Garden Book for Houston and the Texas Gulf Coast.*

Another large garden is that of "Rienzi," the former home of Carroll Sterling and Harris Masterson III, which they donated to the Museum of Fine Arts in 1991. Rienzi, built on Buffalo Bayou, has lovely wooded ravines dotted with azaleas in among other native trees. More formal gardens highlight the azaleas in showy blocks of color.

There are always several additional gardens to visit, and you can tour one, two, or all of them. Each has its own expression of this loveliest of spring flowers, and you just might gain some inspirational ideas that could make your home a candidate for a spot on the Azalea Trail next year. But even if you have less lofty goals, the sheer beauty of these flowers will lift your heart.

Mercer Arboretum March Mart

This is the big one, in time for spring planting—be there early.

Address: 22306 Aldine Westfield Road, Humble TX 77338
Phone: 281-443-8731
Website: www.hcp4.net/mercer
Hours of operation: Friday and Saturday 8:00 A.M.–4:00 P.M., second to last
    weekend in March
Directions: I-45 north to FM 1960, then turn east. Turn left at Aldine West-
    field Road, go 1¼ miles, and turn left at the light into the arboretum or
    right for the visitor center.
Map Location: NS

Everyone knows about the March Mart, where gardeners come from far and near to snap up bargains on a wide variety of unique plants, some of which are from Mercer's own collections of unusual plants. And if you are not sure of the best spot in your garden for that angel's trumpet, experts can help you settle it in so it will blow its horn happily forevermore.

This sale, one of the Gulf Coast's largest, has been held for more than thirty years, so everything runs as smoothly as a new lawn mower. Shuttles will take you from the parking areas to the sale, and a limited number of wagons are available—better to bring your own. You can purchase the very helpful March Mart Plant Guide, more than one hundred pages long, which lists all of the plants available and their culture requirements. This is a gold mine of information for newcomers to the area, as well as seasoned gardeners. For instance, did you know there is a "fiber optic plant" for sale? More than one hundred experts are on hand to advise and answer questions about the plants at the sale or questions about your particular green and growing—or not—garden.

More than two thousand varieties of top-quality plants are available, many of which are not found at your local nursery. There's something in every price range, from the familiar cheery flats of colorful impatiens to the more exotic-looking large tropicals. In many instances, the hard-working Mercer volunteers have propagated these plants from Mercer's own collections or contacted regional growers for those impossible-to-find plants. It's tempting to blow the budget and buy everything in sight.

Highlights at a recent visit to the mart were the huge selection of gingers, including the very striking silver-striped peacock ginger. With eighty varieties of roses available, you will find one or more to fill your garden with scented beauty. In order to introduce gardeners to plants that might not be familiar, each year an annual and a perennial are featured. All kinds of herbs are sold—culinary, medicinal, and ones that are just plain fun, like the lamb's ears, which have soft fuzzy leaves that everyone loves to touch.

When decisions about which shrubs to buy get to be too much, you can revive yourself with tropical-sounding dishes at the Palms Café before setting out again. And when you leave the sale with all of your new finds, you are allowed to choose a packet of seeds as a thank-you for coming. Now *that's* Texas hospitality.

Bulb and Plant Mart

You'd better not miss it!

Address: 5801 San Felipe at Bering (Westminster United Methodist Church), Houston TX 77057
Website: www.gchouston.org
Hours of operation: Thursday and Friday 9:30 A.M.–5.00 P.M.; Saturday 9:30 A.M.–2.00 P.M. in mid-October
Directions: West on San Felipe from Loop 610 west, past Chimney Rock to Bering
Map Location: W2B

Bring your little red wagon, hop in the SUV, and head over to a Houston institution: the annual Bulb and Plant Mart, sponsored by the Garden Club of Houston (GCH). This is a premier event in our town.

Parking and admission are free, and you will receive a free horticultural guide for Houston, written by GCH members, which is very helpful for newcomers and longtime residents alike. Then you're ready to brave the other gardeners who are busily snapping up bargains. If you wish, you can even preorder bulbs (by mid-August) at the website and then pay for them at special times during the sale. The offerings here are fat, top-notch bulbs from the best growers both here and abroad. Garden club members are knowledgeable and very willing to answer your questions about their wares.

For drifts of peach, pink, white, and orange, as well as the more familiar yellow, nothing can beat the more than twenty varieties of daffodils featured at the Bulb Mart. Perhaps the color punch of masses of tulips nodding in the breeze is what you want; if so, there are forty varieties for sale. More than sixty varieties of amaryllis, hyacinths, and narcissus are also offered. Small bulbs are represented, too: dark blue muscari, a rainbow of anemones, ranunculus, and many others. In addition, look for some unique bulbs grown by the club members themselves.

Profits from the sale benefit club beautification projects such as the gardens of the hospice at the Texas Medical Center and at the Museum of Fine Arts. Donations of bulbs to beautify schools, parks, and other public spaces do a lot to brighten our city.

A second aspect of the sale involves plants—specifically, hard-to-find and unusual ones. Houstonians love gingers, and gingers love Houston. Here you will find several varieties that your local nursery might not carry. Moreover, we can grow many types of citrus in Houston, and many people have a lemon or lime tree growing on their patio. The flowers' fragrance is unbelievable, and the added bonus of fruit can add zest to a summer drink or marinade for the grill.

So buy your tulips, pop them into the fridge for eight weeks to fool them into thinking they never left Holland, plant them in December, and enjoy a colorful spring. Or force some paperwhite narcissus to bloom for Christmas fragrance. The ideas are endless.

Nutcracker Market

*Nutcrackers and other festive baubles launch
the holiday season.*

Address: 8400 Kirby Drive, Houston TX 77054 (Reliant Event Center)
Website: www.nutcrackermarket.com
Hours of operation: Thursday and Friday 10:00 A.M.–8:00 P.M.; Saturday and
    Sunday 10:00 A.M.–6:00 P.M. in mid-November
Admission: $10.00 each day or $9.00 in advance at area Randall's stores. Chil-
    dren under 5 are admitted free. Half-price admission is available two hours
    before closing each day. No strollers, carts, or rolling bags are allowed.
Directions: Loop 610 west to Kirby Drive; turn right (north) on Kirby. Follow
    signs to parking.
Map Location: SW1

Deck the halls with all your finds at this annual market, and get in
the mood for the holiday season. Held in mid-November, this huge
event, sponsored by the Houston Ballet Guild, features more than
three hundred vendors with many one-of-a-kind treasures for home
and garden. Proceeds benefit the Houston Ballet and fund many of
its programs to train young dancers.

Yes, you will definitely find colorful nutcrackers at the market.
You'll also see holiday decorations ranging from the bold and beautiful to the charming and whimsical. Looking for a beagle tree orna-
ment for the dog lover on your list? It's here. You can even buy the
tree to hang it on.

If you purchase items from Brookwood Community or the Children's Art Project of M. D. Anderson Hospital, you are helping in a
very special way. Brookwood sells beautiful decorative ceramics,
some with a holiday theme, including crèches, and some featuring
bluebonnets and other Texana. Surely you know some northern
gardener who would love a bluebonnet platter from Texas. These
ceramics are handmade by the Brookwood residents and are top
quality. The children who are at M. D. Anderson for treatment create memorable and very artistic holiday cards and gifts. Some of the
cards are Texas themed, some are light hearted, and some are religious. All of them are exceptional, as are the children who create

them. Sending these Christmas cards has been a Houston tradition for years.

You might wonder about the feeding-frenzy atmosphere at the Donne di Domani booth. Only at the annual Nutcracker Market can you buy the homemade Italian spaghetti sauce that these marvelous Italian women make, and it goes faster than tickets to the Super Bowl.

It's not just holiday items that are for sale; gourmet food, clothing, children's items, furniture, and more are among the many other offerings at the market. You really can do all of your holiday shopping here under one roof.

Farmers' Markets, Pick-It-Yourself Farms, and Christmas Tree Farms

That plea of parents everywhere—"Eat your veggies!"—might be easier to take if the kiddies have picked the green beans or tomatoes themselves. If you go to one of Houston's many pick-it-yourself farms, you will not have to worry about crop yields, fertilizing, watering, or removing giant caterpillars from your tomato crop. Don't want to play Farmer Brown but still want fresh produce? Try something new at one of the farmers' markets springing up around town. Christmas trees, too, are there for the chopping at many locations near Houston.

Month after month of long, sunny days with plentiful rain for irrigation equals a produce-growing climate that is hard to beat. A postage-stamp-sized backyard need not mean foregoing just-picked flavor in veggies and fruits. With an increasing interest in produce picked at its peak, it was inevitable that the pick-it-yourself farms would flourish. Not only do you have produce you have hand-selected, but the price is right, and you can have a good time gathering it.

Children can make a game out of finding the reddest, ripest strawberries peeking out from under the green, leafy plants. Most farms encourage picnics, and some have pumpkin patches and fall harvest festivals. Do call before you go to make sure the produce you want to pick is ripe; harvest times vary yearly.

Another fast-growing option is purchasing your veggies at one of the many farmers' markets. These feature fresh organic produce, locally grown and in season. Not only can you buy your daily bread to complement a dewy-fresh salad, but you can also obtain just-laid eggs, cheeses, condiments, and sauces to perk up any meal. Top everything off with a handmade artisan chocolate, and you'll swear off fast food forever. The vendors are enthusiastic about their wares, offering samples and recipes.

A trip to a farmers' market should not be a one-time excursion. Drop in at your favorite market weekly; the offerings change with the seasons and are always going to be newly picked and delicious. Houstonians have a right to have good fresh organic produce. Your enthusiastic support will mean more and better food for everyone.

Finally, if you have fond memories of heading off to a snowy forest to chop down a Christmas tree, I cannot promise the snow, but you can still chop down the freshest tree available at one of the Christmas tree farms in the area. Most have Virginia pines and Leyland cypress trees ready for harvesting, as well as precut Frazier firs from North Carolina.

Still looking for more? There are visits with Santa, train rides, hayrides to the fields, hot chocolate, and Christmas crafts that make great gifts. Most of the Christmas tree farms gear up around Thanksgiving for the busy season, but opening hours vary. It's best to check the website or call to confirm the hours of operation.

Bayou City Farmers' Market

Farm fresh flavor deep in the heart of Houston

Address: 3000 Richmond (behind the building), Houston TX 77098
Phone: 713-880-5540
Website: www.urbanharvest.org
Hours of operation: Wednesday 4:00 P.M.–7:00 P.M., Saturday 8:00 A.M.–noon
Directions: Richmond, then turn north on Eastside, between Buffalo Speedway and Kirby, turn right into parking lot behind building at 3000 Richmond
Map Location: W1

Farmers' markets are sprouting in Houston like dandelions in a spring lawn. A great addition to the city's burgeoning market scene is the Bayou City Farmers' Market, where a wide variety of items, both edible and crafted, is available: free-range eggs, honey, edible blossoms, savory breads and other baked goods, vegetables and fruits in season at their freshest, flowering plants for your garden, and bouquets of cut flowers ready to go.

Pears and Gorgonzola cheese are a classic pairing, but have you tried pear and Gorgonzola bread? A slice of this treat, plus a cup of tea sweetened with an acacia honey, would jumpstart anyone's day nicely. As you wander from booth to booth, you find yourself coming up with creative inspirations for combining the foods you see.

While all of the many food and nonfood items are tempting, the produce is really the star attraction at a farmers' market. If you do not have room for a sunny, large tomato patch, don't fret: Tomatoes of all kinds are here in abundance, bursting with red-ripe flavor. A Tomato Festival in June celebrates this favorite veggie with tables piled high with the well-known red and yellow varieties, as well as purple, green, orange, brown, and striped tomatoes. In addition to familiar vegetables, you will often see more exotic ones, including Asian, African, and South American varieties that will spice up your meals. Be adventurous and try some; the vendors are happy to suggest ways to prepare them.

When summer comes, stop in and buy some luscious peaches. Nothing is as heavenly as a warm peach pie topped with a scoop of Blue Bell vanilla ice cream. Seasonal blueberries, blackberries, and strawberries will likely inspire you to try cobblers, muffins, and other treats. Citrus in all its many forms grows well here, and the market celebrates it with a Citrus Festival in January.

Having lovingly tended their produce before bringing it to the market, the vendors naturally want you to enjoy it, too. Thus, they are eager to give suggestions, recipes, and even cooking demonstrations to whet your appetite.

We all want the freshest produce, the tastiest baked goods, and the most savory jams and salsas. You'll find them at a local farmers' market, so get out and support their efforts while you enjoy some good eating.

39

Farmers' Markets, Pick-It-Yourself Farms, and Christmas Tree Farms

Blackberries of Houston

Blackberry wine? Why not? It's elegant and tastes good, too.

Address: 19531Cypress Church Road, Cypress TX 77433
Phone: 281-373-5357
Website: blackberriesofhouston.com
Hours of operation: Daily 7:30 A.M.–5:30 P.M.
Directions: SH 290 west to Mueschke Road. Exit and go north two miles,
then turn right onto Cypress Church Road. Go half a mile; the farm is on
the right.
Map Location: NWS

One of summer's sweet delights is a freshly made fragrant blackberry pie warm from the oven, topped with a scoop of vanilla ice cream. However, if you have priced blackberries in the grocery stores lately, you know it costs a lot to buy enough of those little half-pint containers to make a pie. But take heart, for not all is lost. A trip out to the country, to Blackberries of Houston, will fill your freezer with enough of these tasty little black gems to make several pies—or cobblers, cordials, or additions to your morning cereal.

J. D. and Frankie McMaster know how to raise top-quality blackberries. Both are from rural families and for several years owned McMaster's Rice Hull Compost. After they retired, they decided to grow blackberries and now have several acres of them for your enjoyment, as well as acreage devoted to vegetables, which they also sell.

Bring the kids out to the country, and let them see the sources of some of the food they eat. Blackberry picking will go much faster with several hands helping. Best of all, you don't need to worry about scratched hands; these berries are thornless.

When you have enough berries, relax, stroll around the grounds, and enjoy the pretty pond and rose garden. This is a good chance to show children that carrots grow under ground, squash and cucumbers have miniature versions of their veggies attached to the flowers, and peppers come in all colors and shapes. They might even see a fierce-looking tomato hornworm munching away—I hope not.

The McMasters are wine aficionados and make blackberry wine for their own consumption. You'll enjoy talking about wine with them and perhaps sampling a little of their blackberry wine.

Blackberries are usually ready from late May through June, but to be certain, call before you go since sometimes Mother Nature is slow to get things going. Buckets for picking are provided, and payment is by cash only.

You can also take the soil-improving benefits of rice hull compost to your own garden. Bring your own bags or load up the back of the pickup. Either way, your garden will thank you.

Central City Co-Op

Feeding the body, the mind, and the whole community

Address: 2115 Taft Street, Houston TX 77006
Phone: not listed
Website: www.centralcityco-op.org
Hours of operation: Wednesday 9:00 A.M.–6:45 P.M., Saturday 9:00 A.M.–
    1:30 P.M.
Directions: in town, two blocks north of Fairview, east of Montrose, between
    Westheimer and West Gray
Map Location: W1

Central City Co-op is a variation on the farmers' market theme, yet one that still champions fresh-from-the-grower food. The co-op shares space with the Taft Street Coffee House and Strange Land Books, so you can have a cup of organic fair trade coffee, browse through some books, then pick up your fresh produce from the co-op.

Co-ops usually require you to pay a week in advance for varying quantities of vegetables or fruits. You come in the following week to pick up your fresh veggies, which will vary according to what's available. Much, but not all, of the produce is local, but all of it is organically grown. This is so important when you consider that what we put into our mouths should be pesticide free and wholesome. It is heartening to see all the younger families shopping here that believe this is essential. The children enjoy helping to select the produce.

On a given day, you might find all sorts of Asian greens piled high. Be adventurous—buy some. If you are not sure what to do with them when you get them home, ask someone. People here are extremely helpful and want to share their ideas with you.

The website is a treasure trove of recipes: a cactus breakfast burrito is a unique take on this Texas favorite, and coconut nectarine sorbet would be an elegant finale to any meal.

Cooking condiments such as olive oils, sesame tahini, shoyu, cookies, and dried fruits and beans are stocked here to save you an extra trip to a grocery store.

The co-op wants to foster the idea of people coming together not only to have access to healthy organic food but also to form a community where the members help one another. To that end, the website has links to information about diet, exercise, legal and financial matters, education, and other helpful topics. The co-op has organized donations for hurricane and tsunami victims and advertises events elsewhere in the community such as a free tax-preparation day.

If you live elsewhere in the city or suburbs, check the website for other co-ops nearer to where you live. There is no reason you cannot have wholesome organic food, too, no matter where you are.

Christmas Tree Farms

What could be more invigorating than a December day when you feel a nip in the air, and the whole family heads off to a farm to pick out a fresh, Texas-grown Christmas tree? Well, maybe some hot chocolate and cider, a hayride, and Santa would be even better. Bring the camera and create a new family tradition at one of these farms.

Cleveland Area

A&W Christmas Trees, Route 4, Box 1091, Cleveland TX 77327; phone: 281-592-5307

Keith's Christmas Trees, 15174 Highway 1008, Dayton TX 77535; phone: 281-592-5032

Tomball/Spring Area

High Star Christmas Trees, Inc., 19020 Becker Road, Hockley TX 77447; phone: 281-255-9888; website: www.highstar farm.com

Jingle Bell Ranch, 20139 Telge Road, Tomball TX 77377;
 phone: 281-351-5912; website: www.jinglebellranch.com
Old Time Christmas Tree Farm, 7632 Spring Cypress Road,
 Spring TX 77379; phone: 281-370-9141; website:
 www.oldtimechristmastree.com
Spring Creek Growers, 23803 Decker Prairie–Rosehill Road,
 Magnolia TX 77355; phone: 281-259-8114; website:
 www.springcreekgrowers.com
Red Caboose Farm and Christmas Trees, 14558 Tree Farm
 Road, Magnolia TX 77354; phone: 281-252-0159; website:
 www.redcaboosefarmandchristmastrees.com

Alvin Area

Holiday Acres, 9029 Mustang Bayou Road (County Road 95),
 Manvel TX 77578; phone: 281-756-9120; website:
 www.theholidayacres.com

Farmers Marketing Association

Who knew veggies could be so much fun?

Address: 2520 Airline Drive, Houston TX 77009
Phone: 713-862-8866
Hours of operation: Daily 5:30 A.M.–8:30 P.M.
Directions: I-45 north to Cavalcade-Link exit inside Loop 610, west on Cavalcade, north on Airline, on the right
Map Location: N1

Restaurant chefs in Houston do not have to drive to Fredericksburg to get bushel baskets of fresh peaches for their sublime cobblers. They make the short trip up I-45 to the Farmers Marketing Association on Airline Drive. Get there early for the best selection, though. The market opens at 5:30 A.M., and the choicest produce flies out the door.

Peppers of every hue and shape imaginable are on display: red and yellow bell peppers, as well as the more common green ones. Jalapenos, poblanos, Anaheims, scotch bonnets, and flaming little habañeros will sear your sinuses or kick your cuisine up a notch. Snapping-fresh green beans, local red-ripe tomatoes, and other goodies make it a pleasure, not a chore, to get fresh veggies and fruits into all of your meals.

Canino's market is in the front of the market itself. In addition to all kinds of produce, it carries a selection of spices, honeys, and oils to complement the taste of the veggies and fruits you take home.

The independent produce sellers in the back of the market are usually smaller vendors, but they offer a good variety of produce at competitive prices. Especially good bargains are the baskets for a dollar filled with things such as three large eggplants, fresh green beans, or tiny cucumbers for pickling.

Need a quick bouquet of flowers to take along? A florist is situated next to the market. And if the thought of facing shopping for anything that early in the morning makes you weak, you're in luck. There's a good *panadería*, or bakery, next door where you can get freshly baked Mexican pastries of all kinds, or *bolillos*, to stave off your hunger.

Houston Farmers' Market

Fresh food the old-fashioned way: from the farmer

Address: 3106 White Oak Drive, Houston TX 77007
Phone: none listed
Website: www.houstonfarmersmarket.org
Hours of operation: Saturday 8:00 A.M.–noon in the Heights; Tuesday 4:00
    P.M.–7:00 P.M. in the Rice Village area
Directions: The Tuesday afternoon market is in the parking lot nearest
    to Rice stadium at Rice University; the Saturday market is behind
    Onion Creek Coffee House on White Oak between Studewood and
    Heights Boulevard.
Map Location: NW1

Heading for the Heights on Saturday in search of antiques? Why not combine that pleasurable activity with a visit to the Houston Farmers' Market? Stroll around under the shady trees and pick up dewy-fresh veggies for tonight's feast, maybe some delectable pastries or luscious chocolate as a finale, perhaps some fragrant goat's milk soap, too. Then, after all the decisions are made and the shopping bags are full, relax on the shaded patio at the Onion Creek Coffee House with a creamy latte and savor the moment.

Ponder a tomato in your local grocery store. How many days—or even weeks—do you think it has been since that tomato basked in the sun? In contrast, the tomatoes at this market were probably picked yesterday—or even this morning—while at the apex of their juiciness and flavor. Honestly now, which would you prefer? Naturally, you won't find them here in February since they're not in season then, but plenty of other veggies and fruits are.

Year-round, according to the season, the tables are piled high with the liveliest leafy greens, a rainbow of heirloom and old-favorite tomato varieties, tangy citrus, and peppers to satisfy every taste. Summer means fresh local peaches, and they will be here in abundance for fragrant cobblers and delectable peach ice cream or just for devouring while the juice runs down your arm. *Heavenly.*

But you will have more to savor than just produce. A slice from a fragrant loaf of rosemary bread topped with creamy goat cheese and a drizzle of aromatic local honey will inspire dreams of the south of France. To prolong the ambiance, indulge in a bath scented with the fragrance of lavender goat's milk products. Continuing the French theme, an *omelette aux fines herbes* takes little time to assemble using the super-fresh pastured eggs and aromatic herbs that you find here.

Finally, grace your table with a bouquet of fresh-from-the-garden flowers. Then thank your lucky stars that you live in Houston, where you can select from an abundance of many of the tasty foods that make everyday cooking and eating a pleasure rather than a chore. Life is meant to be lived with style; you owe it to yourself to have the very best food available. A good start would be the Houston Farmers' Market on a Saturday morning.

King's Orchard

Strawberries, blackberries, blueberries, and figs
as far as the eye can see

Address: 11282 County Road 302, Plantersville TX 77363
Phone: 936-894-2766
Website: www.kingsorchard.com
Hours of operation: Tuesday–Sunday 8:00 A.M.–5:00 P.M., closed Monday;
    season runs from February to September
Directions: I-45 north to FM 1488 exit, west 18 miles to Magnolia, right on FM
    1774, and go 6¹/₂ miles north. Turn left at orchard sign onto CR 302, and
    go ³/₄ mile.
Map Location: NWS

If you cringe at the thought of paying a king's ransom for a little package of blackberries in the grocery store, then come to the King's Orchard, where you will get a lot more for your money. Yes, you do pick these blackberries, strawberries, blueberries, and figs yourself, but it is relaxing and fun. Relish the quiet out here in the country; all you hear are mockingbirds, robins, woodpeckers, and other music makers. Make the trip a day's outing with the children, and you will be surprised at how fast the picking goes. And the kids can see that blueberries are much more than dried-up little purple pellets in the muffin mix; at this stage they are plump and tasty real fruit.

Acres and acres of berries are at King's Orchard for the picking: strawberries in the spring, then blackberries and blueberries in the summer, ending with figs in late summer. The paths between the rows are wide enough that you won't brush the bushes easily, yet close enough that you can pick from both sides. Moreover, the paths are worn flat by lots of foot traffic, so no boots are needed, just comfortable shoes. It's best to check the website or call to make sure that the fruit you want to pick is available. Sometimes the orchard closes early for the year if all of the fruit has been gathered.

All of the fruit is priced by the pound, and the prices are reasonable. The orchard provides little red wagons to hold the containers for the fruit, which you purchase for a dollar apiece. The fruit is then weighed and put into plastic bags for the trip home. Before you leave, however, be sure to buy a cold drink, relax, and enjoy a picnic lunch in the shade—you've earned it.

This would be a great place to bring a group of children to pick some juicy strawberries, work off some of that amazing kid energy they have in abundance, then go home to feast on strawberry shortcake that they can make themselves: Just buy biscuits and whipped cream, and let the youngsters have a party. And they will learn valuable lessons about good food and where it comes from.

Best of all, think of the blueberry pancakes, strawberry pies, fig preserves, and blackberry cobblers the whole family will savor next winter. King's Orchard also has an acre of flowers that you can cut yourself. This guarantees that you can hand-select the freshest posies that will last the longest. If you prefer not to turn your fruit bounty into jam, the store sells jams, jellies, and other gift items.

Matt Family Orchard, Inc.

Peace in the country, tasty and unusual fruits in the basket

Address: 21110 Bauer Hockley Road, Tomball TX 77377
Phone: 281-351-7676
Website: www.mattfamilyorchard.com
Hours of operation: when fruit is in season, Monday–Saturday 9:00 A.M.– 2:00 P.M., or anytime with reservations; October and November, Sunday noon–4:00 P.M.; reservations are necessary for the harvest festival or group tours
Directions: SH 290 7 miles past FM 1960 to Mueschke Road, exit north on Mueschke, travel 3.2 miles to Bauer Hockley. At the Matt Family Orchard sign, turn west and travel 1 mile, go through the green pipe gate, and go to the green barn.
Map Location: NWS

A friendly gaggle of guinea fowl serves as the avian welcoming committee of the Matt Family Orchard. You know you're in the country now; fruit trees dot the gentle hills, and picnic tables await you.

The sign says "fresh to you as God blesses us," and God has blessed the Matts with acres of productive trees, just waiting for you to pick the very ripest fruit from their branches. Though familiar fruits such as blackberries, figs, and citrus are grown, the orchards also produce more unusual fruits such as jujubes or Asian dates (jujubes are not really palm dates but are actually more closely related to plums and cherries), persimmons, and crisp-fleshed Asian pears.

Mouthwatering recipes are available at the Matt Family Orchard website: How does an Asian pear salad with radicchio and toasted hazelnuts sound? Persimmon recipes abound, so if you have been curious about this decorative orange-red fruit, go ahead and pick some, then go home and experiment. Of course, nothing can match homemade fig preserves slathered on a steaming hot biscuit fresh from the oven.

Once you have picked the ripest fruit, take a well-deserved break, and spread out a picnic under the shade trees. The tables seat a hundred hungry picnickers, plenty of space for a reunion or a school outing.

The Harvest Festival in October is bound to be fun for all. Choose your own pumpkin from the pumpkin patch, get creative and dress up a scarecrow, or enjoy a hayride out in the fresh air. A huge haystack invites the kids to climb and slide on it. Campfires can warm up the air if the day is chilly. Deer, foxes, rabbits, and other wildlife might be curious enough to make a special appearance, so keep an eye open for them.

Midtown Farmers' Market

The very best seasonal produce and delectable prepared food

The
Garden Lover's
Guide to
Houston

Address: 3701 Travis Street, Houston TX 77002
Phone: 713-524-6922
Website: www.tafia.com
Hours of operation: Saturday 8:00 A.M. to noon
Directions: On Travis Street, one block north of Alabama, at the corner of Winbern
Map Location: W1

For Monica Pope, whose cooking philosophy embraces the use of seasonal foods, becoming a founder of the Midtown Farmers' Market was a natural outgrowth of her passion for such food from nearby sources. The market, located adjacent to her successful restaurant, t'afia, offers a cornucopia of locally grown produce, as well as an assortment of appetizing prepared foods.

Where to begin? The essence of this market is that you will find the freshest produce appropriate to the current season. In January, that means juicy sweet citrus from growers near Houston, rather than strawberries, which travel all the way from South America, losing their freshness en route. A wave of greens spills over the counter, and you can bet they are all bursting with vitamins and flavor. The produce may not always be the picture-perfect kind found in supermarkets, but the flavor and goodness are incomparable.

Want basil? Dewy-fresh green and purple bunches glow in the summer sun, ready to complement the season's huge variety of tomatoes. The jewel tones of rows of jams and relishes sparkle, tempting you to use them to accent your dishes.

Lest you think that all of the food is of the veggie variety, stroll around and see some of the other offerings. You won't be able to resist the heavenly aromas wafting from the Kraftsmen Baking Company's stand. Croissants, scones, breads bursting with flavor, and luscious pastries are available. And I dare you to walk by Brown Paper Chocolates without stopping and buying. Though some of us think that chocolate is one of the major food groups, it actually does contain antioxidants, which are helpful in the fight against disease. So enjoy—in moderation.

Don't have time to cook or want some sauces to pep up your dishes? Chef Pope's "plum" good cooking can help you out. The Plum Pantry selection of sauces and marinades may be just what you need to change your meals from ho-hum to awesome. If you are really in a time crunch, Plum Easy will provide you with scrumptious meals to go, all with Monica Pope's artistic touch. Finally, as you leave, choose a bouquet from a rainbow of fresh-cut flowers to grace your table.

49

Farmers'
Markets, Pick-It-
Yourself Farms,
and Christmas
Tree Farms

Moorhead's Blueberry Farm

Enjoy a summers' day, then enjoy the fruits of your labor.

Address: 19531 Moorhead Road, Conroe TX 77302
Phone: 281-572-1265 or 888-702-0622
Website: www.moorheadsblueberryfarm.com
Hours of operation: Daily 7:00 A.M.–9:00 P.M.
Directions: Take US 59 north out of the city to FM 1314, then go west; turn
    left onto Calhoun Road, left onto East Drive, right onto Walker Road, and
    left onto Moorhead Road to the farm.
Map Location: NS

What could be tastier on a Saturday morning than a stack of steaming hot pancakes dotted with plump, tasty blueberries? How about a deep dish blueberry pie, bursting with fruit, and a scoop of ice cream melting on top? Yummy.

Rustic signs with arrows and blueberries lead you along winding roads to Moorhead's Blueberry Farm. For years, Houstonians have been able to drive to the country and pick buckets of blueberries to turn into fragrant pies, cobblers, and jams.

Several varieties of southern Rabbiteye blueberries grow and mature at different times, so there are always plenty of berries to pick during the season, which generally runs from the last weekend in May to mid-July. Call before you go, at the beginning and end of the season, to make sure the berries are ready. It's comforting to know that no pesticides are used on these berries.

The first stop is to pick up buckets, which they provide. Even the littlest toddler can pick since the berries are scattered thickly on five-foot-tall bushes with no thorns. A real plus is that you can sample as many berries as you want while you wander up and down the rows (people come to check out with telltale contented purple grins). The staff transfers your berries to plastic bags for weighing; the cost per pound is $1.50, definitely cheaper than buying those little cartons at the store.

As you mosey around the grounds, picking a few berries, eating a few more, the only sounds you hear will be the liquid songs of cardinals and thrushes or the drumming of a woodpecker. Ah, peace.

The
Garden Lover's
Guide to
Houston

Pack up a picnic lunch, so that when you are through picking, you can relax at the picnic area. Cold sodas and water are available, as are restrooms.

Blueberries are high on the list of good things to eat that are also good for you. That deep blue color means loads of antioxidants, so pop a few in your mouth, and know you're doing your body a favor.

The Market Street Farmers' Market

*Homegrown, homemade, and handmade goodies
in the Woodlands*

Address: Market Street, The Woodlands TX 77380
Phone: 281-419-4774
Website: www. marketstreet-the woodlands.com
Hours of operation: Saturday 8:00 A.M.–11:00 A.M. from April to June 30
Directions: I-45 or Hardy Toll Road to Woodlands Parkway exit. Follow the
    signs to the Cynthia Woods Mitchell Pavilion, then signs to Market Street,
    which is across from the pavilion.
Map Location: NWS

If you live in The Woodlands, there is no need to drive all the way to Houston any more for farm-fresh treats. The Market Street Farmers' Market can supply you with appetizing edibles for your family—and that includes Fido and Muffin, too.

It is always a pleasure to have fresh veggies and fruits. The waxy cucumbers full of large seeds from the supermarket can't hold a candle to a thin-skinned tender cuke from the market. And it goes without saying that a tomato will be a hedonistic delight rather than a teeth-gnashing disappointment when you bite into it.

To go a step further, why not pair that tomato and cucumber with some plain or herbal goat cheese? Add a few basil leaves, tear off chunks of some of the fragrant whole-grain bread sold here, and you will have a summertime treat that's easy on the waistline, too. Grab a fresh floral bouquet or an orchid or two and some soy candles to set the mood while you're at it.

Craving heartier fare? You can find locally raised, grass-fed beef

Farmers' Markets, Pick-It-Yourself Farms, and Christmas Tree Farms

for sale. Grill and serve it with one of the many savory or peppery sauces and condiments available from the market vendors. They can even sharpen the knives you use to carve the beef.

If your image of a goat is that of a smelly beastie on grandpa's farm that would butt anything in sight, think again. Today's goats have had an image makeover. Not only can goat's milk be transformed into sublime tangy cheeses, but it can also yield soaps and lotions that are gentle to the skin and delicately scented with lavender, lemon verbena, and other delicate fragrances.

Let's not forget our four-legged friends; they appreciate homemade goodies, too. Give them the satisfaction of chewing on a mail carrier or UPS delivery person—not the real thing but a tasty cookie to gnaw instead. The treats look good enough for humans to eat. A kitty might appreciate a crocheted catnip mouse to bat around.

As at all of the farmers' markets in our area, the vendors are eager to answer your questions about their produce and other items. They are at the markets because they want to introduce you to foods and other products that are local and made in small batches by people who care about what they are selling. You will be glad you supported them.

Day Trips

hen you simply must get out of town, here are some great ideas for a quick escape. Parks, gardens, and nurseries all beckon you to enjoy a change of scenery—and beautiful scenery at that. These garden destinations can be either the reason for your day trip or part of a weekend minivacation that recharges your batteries for the week ahead at work.

This chapter focuses on three distinct regions. The first excursion is to the area south of Houston, excluding Galveston, which is another separate outing. The third destination is the rural area north and west of Houston. These snapshots of a few locales are by no means exhaustive; rather, they are meant to give you the flavor of the area, along with tourist activities for the whole family. Each of the garden locations is described in detail, following the format for the rest of the destinations in this book. Who knows, you might happen upon a lovely little park, garden, or nursery tucked away in a small town that might become your reason for a jaunt.

Do not forget the extensive chain of state parks scattered across the state. They usually have available a wide range of activities including fishing, bird watching, swimming, and camping. Consider hosting a family reunion at a state park; there is something for everyone in the great outdoors.

South of Houston

Your van is full of family members who are all clamoring to go to places that interest them. So, what's near to Houston and can enthrall the gardener, the techno geek, the sailor, the outdoor café aficionado, and the kids, too? South of Houston, the greater Clear Lake area has it all and then some.

Towns to the south have much to offer, if you prefer not to go all the way to Galveston. Space shuttles and sailboats in the Clear Lake area are a nice combination, but when you crave simple and peaceful relaxation, take a walk on the wild side at Armand Bayou. Reconnect with nature, exploring on foot as you wander along the boardwalk that winds through the woods; you could also glide along the bayou in a canoe or the "Bayou Ranger" pontoon boat. Instead of beach bunnies and surfers, you will see real bunnies and other wildlife.

Alligators reign at Brazos Bend State Park, where you can learn all about them in an informative exhibit. And there is even more to explore here. Bird watching is very rewarding since more than 270 species of birds have been sighted in the area. Teach your little ones the fun of catching their own fish at a dock on one of the lakes. Or just quietly observe the wildlife through a pair of binoculars.

In May, head south to Alvin and stop at Shimek's Gardens for a burst of sun-drenched color. The gardens are devoted to the not-so-humble daylily, and you will be amazed at the huge variety of colors and forms these dazzling flowers can assume. When floral inspiration strikes, longtime nurseries such as Lynn's in League City and Maas in Seabrook can cater to your every need. And remember to stop by Froberg's Farm on the way home for some just-picked fruit and veggies or condiments that will make your meals sing.

A host of other attractions in the area will keep everyone entertained. One of the best known is the National Aeronautics and Space Administration, or NASA. Everyone knows NASA, thanks to memorable moments that have often kept us riveted to our TVs: The first moon landing in 1969 and the dramatically resolved Apollo 13 crisis brought the scientists of NASA into our living rooms. We could only wonder how they guided the spaceships that ranged hundreds of thousands of miles away from us on earth and what technology kept humans alive in deep space conditions.

The mystery and adventure of space have attracted young and old ever since, and a tour of NASA appeals to all ages. Seeing the Mission Control room, the scene of so many important moments in our space program, fascinates the adults. Children and adults alike enjoy exploring labs that simulate many of the conditions found in space, such as weightlessness.

If your children dream of commanding a space shuttle, they can do so at the Kids' Space Place. Interactive exhibits allow them to ride a lunar rover and experience what it is like to live in space. You can even take a virtual tour of the real space station in a mock-up that you enter through a tunnel and experience the sense of motion that you would have in the actual space station high above earth.

Another option for outdoor fun in the sun is Clear Lake Park. Its location on Clear Lake means that water sports are the main attraction. Share your children's delight as they catch their own fish from the fishing piers. Baseball diamonds and picnicking facilities round out a relaxing day.

Want to feel the wind on your face as you skim over the lake but don't have a boat to call your own? Clear Lake has the third largest population of pleasure boats in the United States, and boating is a way of life here, so you can rent anything from a wave runner to a sixty-foot yacht and everything in between. Why not leave the driving to someone else and fish from a charter boat?

Kemah and Seabrook used to be quiet, laid-back towns where Houstonians could watch the fishing boats slowly motor by and at the same time dine on seafood that a short time before had been swimming in Galveston Bay. Seabrook is still peaceful, which explains its appeal for almost three hundred species of birds that inhabit the area's diverse ecosystems. The town is located right on the Great Texas Coastal Birding Trail, so birdwatchers will not be disappointed.

Seabrook's boisterous sibling, Kemah, now has the Kemah Boardwalk, with its scenic lure of waterfront attractions for young and old.

It is a kaleidoscope for the senses: Jugglers amaze, children tumble around on kid-friendly playgrounds and splash in the "dancing fountains," bands play, the Ferris wheel whirls, and the carousel goes around merrily, while a train wends its way around the area.

If all this sounds like way too much activity for you, take in the scene from the vantage point of one of the many waterfront restaurants clustered nearby on the boardwalk. The main attraction is the Aquarium Restaurant, which features, naturally, a fifty-thousand-gallon aquarium in which a hundred species of tropical fish swish through the water while the diners watch them. What the fish think of people dining on their brethren has not been recorded.

Born to shop? You'll find your calling here. Unique among the usual attractions of resort shopping, one store, the Toy Crossing, focuses its attention on trains. Little ones who cannot get enough of Thomas the Tank Engine can persuade their indulgent grandmas to spring for just one more toy. For their parents, Lionel trains bring back memories of long-ago Christmases.

For thrills of the watery kind, take a ride on Joe's Boardwalk Beast. Not a monster that roams the boardwalk, the "beast" is a twenty-five-minute, action-packed but safe ride on a fiercely decorated speedboat that makes a pirate ship look wimpy. The crewmembers promise you that you will get wet one way or the other, even if it's in a water gun game.

There are as many places to stay in the Clear Lake area as there are boats dotting the water. A convenient spot for seeing the sights at NASA is the Nassau Bay Hilton, across from NASA. You can keep your head in the clouds with their parasailing rentals or rent a jet ski for a lively ride on the lake.

In Kemah, the Kemah Boardwalk Inn, with its waterfront views, would be the natural choice. From your private balcony, you can watch all the happenings on the boardwalk.

The Clear Lake area focuses on the sky and the sea, two very different realms. Your whole family will have a wonderful time exploring both of them.

A warm, whimsical greeting at Another Place in Time.

Ceramic birds and frogs are ready for a splash in this birdbath from The Arbor Gate.

These birdhouses from Brookwood Community are almost too pretty for the birds.

Prickly but majestic describes this imposing specimen at Cactus King.

Show your Lone Star pride with pottery from Brookwood Community.

A great use for all those old LPs—the giant roach at Cactus King.

▶ Burgeoning baskets of bougainvillea are a specialty at Congo Nursery.

A naturalistic waterfall from Garden Accents appears to have always been here.

A cat shares the garden with butterflies at the fanciful entry to Garden Mystiques.

Bright yellow flowers of a Brazilian plume plant from Jerry's Jungle Garden light up even the shadiest spot.

Unusual red mussaenda flowering plant from Jerry's Jungle Gardens.

Showy red spikes of fireman's cap like these from Joshua's Native Plants are sure to attract hummingbirds.

Serene blue pottery inspires sentiments to match at Nelson Water Gardens.

The well-designed habitat garden at Joshua's Native Plants is a paradise for birds and butterflies.

► Lit with twinkling lights, a rustic dresser at Lucia's Garden is filled with treasures to pamper both body and soul.

►▼ A hen surveys the passing scene at RCW Nurseries.

►▼▼ Make a bold statement with one-of-a-kind containers and plants from Thompson + Hanson.

Lush greenery enticingly displayed in front of the gift shop at Thompson + Hanson.

Something must have surprised this topiary giraffe at the River Oaks Plant House.

An unusual white variant of the more familiar magenta American beautyberry at Pineywoods Nursery.

They'd look right at home on the veldt, but these topiary animals reside at River Oaks Plant House near Buffalo Speedway.

A chick magnet
at Wabash Antiques
and Feed Store.

Unusual curly bird's nest fern at Another Place in Time.

Armand Bayou Nature Center

Peaceful and natural, and the camp programs
are great for the kids.

Address: 8500 Bay Area Boulevard, Pasadena, TX 77507
Phone 281-474-2551
Website: www.abnc.org
Hours of operation: Tuesday–Saturday 9:00 A.M.–5:00 P.M., Sunday noon–
    5:00 P.M.; closed Monday. Last admission at 4:00 P.M.
Admission: adults, $3; children ages 5–17, $1; children 4 and under, free
Directions: I-45 south from Houston, exit 26 at Bay Area Boulevard. East 7
    miles; nature center is just after Bay Area Park.
Map Location: SES

Big, well-fed squirrels greet you at the beginning of the six-hundred-foot boardwalk that meanders through the trees at Armand Bayou Nature Center. No wonder the squirrels are so fat and sassy—several birdfeeders nearby cater to them, as well as to the many bird species that frequent the center. If you tiptoe quietly, you might see deer, raccoons, armadillos, turtles, and other wildlife. Learn even more about them from the informative signs posted along the trail. At the end of the path, an observation house is home to displays of fish, snakes, and other denizens of the area. When I visited, the children crowded around, telling me excitedly about everything they had seen.

This is a mecca for school groups, scout programs, children's birthday parties, canoe boat trips, stargazers, and bird watchers. Armand Bayou's stated mission is "to reconnect people with nature," and it certainly lives up to its goal. Until the nineteenth century, Native American tribes lived here, and the area, now managed by Harris County, is preserved in a natural state.

Magnificent red-tailed hawks sit regally in their cage at the raptor exhibit, and in the bird blind, you can stay hidden while observing the birds. Armand Bayou is on the Central Flyway, and you will see migrating birds in season. Children can watch the bison from a platform built to observe those animals.

At Martyn Farm (open on Saturdays and Sundays only), families can get a feel for life on an old farm of the 1900s. Here you can

57

Day Trips

observe demonstrations of farm-related activities, such as rope making and other farm chores. Imagine—no computers or dishwashers back then. There is also a woodworking shop, windmill, barn, and garden.

Tell the kids to go take a hike—along five miles of trails winding through the three ecosystems here: forest, bayou, and tall-grass prairie. Reserve a pontoon boat or canoe for yet another way to explore the preserve.

Volunteer opportunities abound, and the volunteers are enthusiastic and well trained. They run the popular camp programs, teach, help restore the habitat, maintain the gardens, and much more.

Brazos Bend State Park
Only an hour away from the city, but a totally different world

Address: 21901 FM 762 Road, Needville TX 77461
Phone: 1-979-553-5101
Website: www.brazosbend.org
Hours of operation: Monday–Thursday 8:00 A.M.–10:00 P.M., Friday–Sunday
    7:00 A.M.–10:00 P.M.
Admission: adults and children 13 and over, $4.00; children 12 and under, free
Directions: South on SH 288 from Houston to Rosharon, then west on FM
    1462 to the park
Map Location: SWS

"Ye Olde Gator Shoppe" is an unusual name for a gift shop, but it does celebrate one of the best-known inhabitants of Brazos Bend State Park. Outside, there are caution signs warning visitors not to approach or feed the gators. Look around, but you might not see them if they are hiding in the water.

Wildflowers, blooming shrubs, and a "butterfly and hummingbird crossing" sign greet you at the park entrance. At the Visitor's Center (open on weekends) you can see treats such as a hummingbird nest with its tiny eggs, plus spiders and slithery snakes to delight the reptile lover. Look down and check out the various animal footprints on the floor.

A "touch table" displays turtle shells, animal skulls, and snakeskins. Kids can listen to birdcalls, learn about wolves from an informative chart, and see bats, armadillos, bugs, squirrels, and taxidermied raccoons and foxes.

A room devoted to alligators, complete with a large gator skeleton, tells you all you need to know about this reptile with the toothy smile. It is hard to imagine an alligator as a loving mommy, but they are very caring and protective of their babies. Gators with their short legs are adequate over land, but they are definitely more at home in the water, where they glide languidly through the water.

Once in the park itself, you will be amazed at the quiet. The trills of birds pierce the air, woodpeckers rat-a-tat in the trees, and if you listen, you can hear small animals stirring in the underbrush. This is a great place to escape the city noise and feel close to nature. You might even see some feral hogs galloping across the road in search of food. Look from the safety of your car, and stay well away from them.

If the idea of waking up to birdsong attracts you, get away from it all and reserve a campsite here. Take the kids fishing at one of the lakes, bike along the Creekfield Lake nature trail, have a dinner flavored with outdoor air, and enjoy nature's beauty.

What could be a better way to recharge your batteries and show nature's wonders to your kids? If you have stars in your eyes, George Observatory is here, too, where a large telescope brings the wonders of the universe nearer to you.

Froberg's Vegetable and Fruit Farm
Fresh from the farm to you

Address: 11875 County Road 190, Alvin TX 77511
Phone: 281-585-3531
Website: none listed
Hours of operation: Daily 9:00 A.M.–6:00 P.M.
Directions: SH 288 to SH 6 exit, go east toward Alvin for 5 miles. Turn right onto CR 99, then left onto CR 190. Be alert when going over the private railroad tracks.
Map Location: SS

Froberg's has been a mainstay in the Alvin area since 1936, but people come here from all over to buy farm-fresh produce. At one time, you could pick your own strawberries and veggies, but now the employees do it for you. A testament to the farm's popularity is that the shop is filled with customers at all times. You can buy tomatoes, peppers, flowers, and herbs to plant, but why bother? Much easier to let someone else raise the veggies, and you pick them up in the cool of the produce store at Froberg's.

The folks here get creative with the fruits of their labors and the vegetables, too. Have you tried a pear mincemeat pie? Or how about some pear marmalade on an English muffin? When was the last time you had pickled okra or pickled beets? Everyone's grandma used to make these; Froberg's still does. Of course, they also make heavenly strawberry jams and preserves, as well as all kinds of sauces and marinades.

A homemade farm-fresh pie is the perfect ending to a meal starring some of Froberg's vegetables. A scrumptious strawberry pie would be perfect, but there are other choices as well, all brimming with good things and baked right here at the farm.

But not by veggies alone do we live. Froberg's usually offers a selection of convenient items that you just can't do without. Crocheted Easter baskets in a rainbow of colors are filled with goodies to charm any child. A rustic basket shaped like the state of Texas would make an attractive gift when filled with some of the gourmet food offerings for sale here.

At Froberg's, the produce you buy is homegrown in season. If you do not have the room or the inclination to raise your own vegetables and fruits, go to Froberg's Vegetable and Fruit Farm instead. And do try one of the strawberry pies.

Lynn's Landscaping and Water Garden Center
As welcoming as wandering through a friend's garden

Address: 2060 Pecan Orchard Road, League City TX 77573

Phone: 281-332-4651

Website: www.lynnslandscaping.com

Hours of operation: Monday–Saturday 9:30 A.M.–6:30 P.M., Sunday 9:00 A.M.– 5:30 P.M.

Directions: I-45 south, exit FM 518, east to Hwy 3, south to SH 96, turn right and go to Pecan Orchard, turn south to nursery.

Map Location: SES

Entering Lynn's Landscaping through the grass tiki hut gateway puts you in a happy mood right away. Once inside, you will see very attractive nursery stock obviously brimming with health. Lynn's is a friendly, smaller-scaled sort of nursery. Here there are no long tables filled with plants as far as the eye can see. What you will find are smaller, more navigable tables with greenery in attractive groupings.

Winding paths take you past several eye-catching displays that dot the area and give the nursery the air of someone's beloved garden rather than a place to buy plants. Everything is spread out under the sheltering branches of huge oak trees, which adds even more to the air of a garden. There is even a shaded porch overlooking the pond in back, where you can enjoy a break from the sun and survey the surroundings.

Keep walking; there's more to see. Lynn's is noted for water gardens, and a large display pond complete with real koi and an unreal alligator beckons. Two concrete kiddies dangle their feet in the water, oblivious to the alligator. If you do not have room for a large pond, a smaller fountain sends water splashing quietly over two tall cobalt blue containers to a bed of rounded river rocks. Just looking at it will calm you.

The folks who work here are extremely friendly and helpful possibly as a result of working in such pleasing surroundings.

It will be love at first sight for the golfers in your family when they behold the putting green that can find a happy home in your own backyard. It is easy to improve your short game when you only have to walk out the back door to practice.

To complement your garden, gaze at the colorful gazing balls, spring for a fountain, and furnish your garden rooms with some outdoor furniture.

Maas Nursery and Landscaping

You never know what you'll find around the next corner, but you'll love whatever it is.

Address: 5511 Todville Road, Seabrook TX 77586

Phone: 281-474-2488

Website: www.maasnursery.com

Hours of operation: Monday–Saturday 9:00 A.M.–5:00 P.M., Sunday 10:00 A.M.–5:00 P.M. in winter; closes at 6:00 P.M. in summer.

Directions: I-45 south to NASA I exit, go east until road crosses SH 146 and
    becomes Second Street. Go to the end, turn left onto Todville Road, go
    north until you see the nursery.
Map Location: SES

Two giant dogs greet you at the entrance to Maas Nursery. Although
protective in appearance, these are Chinese ceramic Foo dogs, and
they give you a hint of the curiosities that await you.

Maas, which covers fourteen acres, has been an institution in the
Clear Lake area for years. Not only a plant nursery, it's more like a
gigantic estate sale, full of attractive decorative items to beguile you.

Where to begin? You might turn a corner and see a huge black
elephant, looking very much at home underneath the lush vegetation. Buddha gazes serenely down upon a garden spot, and Hindu
statues give an oriental look to the garden. Even Babylonian statuary, reminiscent of Nineveh, dot the gardens. Assyrian griffons and
a five-foot-tall lion share a spot in the jungle. Wander down a shady
allée and see more creatures.

The analogy to an estate sale also means that treasures are not
necessarily laid out in an orderly fashion. Part of the fun is strolling
here and there and appreciating what you see. You never know what
will be around the next corner. It might be a pretty blue wall hanging of fruits and veggies for your kitchen or an eye-catching little tile
table for the patio.

The gentle splash of water follows you wherever you walk. There
are loads of ideas for adding fountains and ponds and the means to
create your own oasis of cool. And, if you get tired from seeing all
there is to see, you can relax at the tables provided and have a picnic
lunch.

Now that you have found the perfect decorative items for the
garden, how about some plants to put in or around them? Maas is,
of course, a nursery and a very well-stocked one. Everything is
available here, from azaleas to zingiber—that's ginger to you and
me. And if you are unsure what kind of TLC your new green purchase needs, just ask the helpful nursery personnel.

Shimek's Gardens

A peaceful and welcoming haven of beauty

Address: 3122 County Road 237, Alvin TX 77511

Phone: 281-331-4395

Website: www.hal-pc.org/~neshimek

Hours of operation: annual spring open house in May; at other times, call for appointment

Directions: SH 6 to Business 35, turn right. At curve, road becomes Davis Bend. Continue west three miles, and turn right onto CR 283. CR 237 is the first left; go .5 miles, gardens on right.

Map Location: SS

In mid-May, when the daylilies are at their peak, Shimek's Gardens are a glorious sight to behold. The Shimeks invite you to see these lovelies for yourself at an annual open house, so, for a memorable experience, stop at the home with the wrought iron daylily sign.

Shimek's is a National Display Garden for the American Hemerocallis Society. Representing the high point of daylily cultivation, these gardens are intended to educate the public about these versatile flowers.

To be designated a National Display Garden, the garden must have a huge number of daylily cultivars—the Shimeks have about 850—representing the labor of hybridizers all over the country and including many of their own cultivars. It goes without saying that the daylilies must be well cared for, so they show their best. Since the gardens are meant to inform gardeners, they must be open for visitors at the peak of bloom. Informative plant markers are part of the equation, too. After all, what good would it be if you did not know the name of that gorgeous pink bicolor daylily that has captured your fancy?

Attractively laid out, the gardens are a pleasure to stroll through. The daylilies are nestled in long beds around four feet across, so it is easy to enjoy each daylily's unique charms up close. Huge old trees are a nice vertical counterpoint to the daylilies hugging the ground. The trunks of a couple of dead trees have been pruned and left in place as graceful natural sculptures to adorn the grounds.

These gardens show off more than a dazzling variety of daylilies,

63

however. Crape myrtles add another, taller layer of flowers with their crinkly blooms. Roses are everywhere, completing the lush blooming scene, as well as adding their scent to the warm air.

This labor of love has evolved into a showplace, dedicated to the memory of the Shimeks' daughter. There could be no finer way of remembering someone than this exceptionally tranquil and gorgeous garden.

Galveston Area

Humans spent eons crawling out of the sea, and now it seems we are always crawling toward it again. When Houstonians crave some waves, Galveston is only fifty miles away—just a short hop down the Gulf Freeway to the sun and surf. Pelicans and seagulls swoop across the sparkling marshes; you go up and over the bridge, and there you are. Years ago, Glen Campbell sang of hearing Galveston's waves crashing and watching its seabirds flying in the sun. Sunning and listening to the soothing crash of the waves are the reasons many people come to Galveston, but if you are not a sun worshipper, there is still plenty to keep both parents and children happy.

The distinctive sparkling pyramids of Moody Gardens loom over the island like their namesakes near Cairo. However, these pyramids honor life, not death. The one of most interest to gardeners houses a biologically diverse rainforest environment, another contains an aquarium with a variety of creatures of the sea, and the third explores the wonders of science by means of interactive exhibits. All of them are worth the time spent there.

The Rainforest Pyramid offers a fascinating look at the flora and fauna of these ecologically important tropical areas. We are now learning that it is essential to preserve the bounty of the rainforests for the benefit of the earth and for our descendants.

While in Galveston, be sure to visit Tom's Thumb Nursery, which specializes in plantings that thrive in spite of the daily dose of salt wafting through the air. Garden and home décor items here often have a nautical theme to complement your beach furnishings.

In the late nineteenth century, the biggest city in Texas was

Galveston, a busy port but possessing civilized amenities such as the state's first opera house, medical school, and newspaper. All are still flourishing today. Victorian, Moorish, and Gothic design elements are blended in the city's unique architecture; outstanding examples include Ashton Villa, the Bishop's Palace, and the Sacred Heart Cathedral.

The hurricane of 1900 changed the face of Galveston forever. Ten thousand people died, and the devastation on the island was widespread, though many of the older structures survived. For a riveting and readable account of everyday life on the island before and after the storm, read *Isaac's Storm* by Erik Larson.

Galveston has come back, but not as the bustling port it once was. Now the slower pace of life invites tourists to play on its beaches, celebrate its festivals, cherish its historical buildings, and learn about the marine environment.

There are many ways to see the town other than by car. Old-fashioned trolleys run from the Strand shopping area to the seawall and around the downtown area. Renting a bike is a great way to move around easily and see the sights. A horse-drawn carriage ride around the East End or the Strand lets you enjoy the stately Victorian architecture at a leisurely pace.

One of the best rides has to be the free twenty-minute ferry ride from Galveston to Bolivar Peninsula. You can park your car, then head topside to watch dolphins arcing in the foamy wake. And check out the amphibious duck boat tours for a unique view of this city by the sea.

There's more: Ridefilm and IMAX theaters that put you right into an onscreen adventure, a nostalgic trip on a paddle wheeler, a chilly spin on an ice rink, or a cooling dip into the crystal-clear waters at Palm Beach. Adjacent to Moody Gardens is a new Schlitterbahn water park that is usable year-round, offering any kind of water activity your kids can imagine. They can zoom down the slides, get chills and thrills from the water coasters, go tubing, shoot the rapids, and even surf some waves. Moody Gardens Hotel is conveniently nearby, if seeing and doing everything in one day is too much.

In case you think all is sun and sand here, you can explore Galveston's cultural side, too. A long-standing tradition is ArtWalk, held every six weeks on a Saturday night. Galleries throw open their doors for special late hours and offer refreshments, with the goal of introducing more people to exciting new art.

Prefer the theater arts? The restored 1894 Opera House, thought to be one of the best of its kind, presents a variety of performances ranging from Broadway plays to dance and classical concerts. Galveston Isle Musicals, located at the Moody Gardens Convention Center, also hosts professionally staged Broadway productions. In the heart of the Strand district, the Strand Theater is the venue for even more stage and musical presentations.

If you are an aviation buff, take a step back in time to World War II days, and admire the collection of planes from this era at the Lone Star Flight Museum. These planes have been lovingly restored to flightworthy condition and depict the development of aviation from its beginnings in Kitty Hawk.

Galveston has its own tall ship, the *Elissa*, a cargo ship from the nineteenth century. This magnificent vessel from our maritime past has been fully restored to its former glory. Each year the *Elissa* is taken out for sea trials off Galveston. The nineteen sails fill with the wind as the ship moves majestically across the water, a reminder of the beauty of the tall ships that once ruled the waves so gracefully.

When Texans mention Mardi Gras, they are likely to be referring to the famous celebration in Galveston that rivals the one in New Orleans. Colorful floats parade majestically past the euphoric crowds of merrymakers who are having the time of their lives as they catch the glittering beads tossed from the floats. At that time of year, Galveston is most definitely not a sleepy little town. In fact, *no* one sleeps during Mardi Gras.

The cool weather of early December evokes the chilly atmosphere of Victorian London for the Dickens on the Strand festival. The Victorian buildings of the Strand are the perfect setting for visitors and performers alike, who are dressed in clothes that hark back to nineteenth-century England. Gas lights flicker, and the warm aroma of roasting chestnuts mingles with that of spiced cider to further the illusion that you are in Dickensian London. Bagpipers, bobbies, magicians, and even the queen herself parade around and perform for you. The celebration takes place on the first weekend in December and has daytime family events, as well as evening ones.

Given Galveston's location, you would expect the seafood to be

The
Garden Lover's
Guide to
Houston

fresh and delicious here, and you would not be wrong. The best shrimp and oyster po'boys in town are at the corner of Thirty-ninth and O streets, at the Shrimp and Stuff Restaurant. If you are driving back to Houston, stop into a seafood store at pier 21, and pick up some shrimp right off the shrimp boats.

Whether your sojourn is just a day or extends to a week, you won't run out of things to do in Galveston. And all of it is accompanied by the rhythmic crash of waves, the tang of salty air, and the cries of the gulls. You will reenter the urban world refreshed and relaxed.

Moody Gardens
Rain or shine, a great alternative to the Galveston beach scene

Address: One Hope Boulevard, Galveston TX 77554
Phone: 800-582-4673
Website: www.moodygardens.com
Hours of operation: Sunday–Friday 10:00 A.M.–6:00 P.M., Saturday 10:00 A.M.–8:00 P.M. Last admission one hour before closing
Admission: adults, $9.95; children 4–12 years, $7.95; under 4 years, free
Directions: I-45 south, exit Sixty-first Street in Galveston. Right on Sixty-first Street and again on Seawall Boulevard. Right on Eighty-first Street to Jones Road. Left on Hope Boulevard to Moody Gardens.
Map Location: SES-Galveston

Galveston's answer to Egypt's pyramids appears as you approach the Moody Gardens complex. These airy, colorful habitats do not house mummies but rather all sorts of natural wonders ready for your child's exploration. You approach the ten-story clear glass Rainforest Pyramid along a beautifully landscaped walkway that will get you in the mood to see some ecological wonders.

Once you are inside the pyramid, a bevy of posters tells you all about the rainforest and advises you to listen to the sounds you'll hear and look up often into the canopy above. A rainforest is different from a jungle in that the canopy in a rainforest is dense and does not let a lot of light through. The knowledgeable docents are eager to answer your questions and even point out little creatures that you might have missed.

Minnesotans fleeing the January snows will appreciate the rain-

forest's steamy ambiance. Plants, animals, and birds from the rainforests of the Americas, Africa, and Asia are represented here in a carefully constructed layering of vegetation, just as you would find in the wild. A theme runs through the exhibit: "What have we got to lose?" The answer is, quite a lot. By razing the rainforests, we destroy medicines, foods, irreplaceable animal and plant species, and much more.

Spectacular rainbow parrots screech at the red ibis stalking around, while graceful golden koi swimming in a pond mesmerize the children watching them. Bats are nocturnal, so the glassed-in bat cave is dimly lit. Therefore, it is easy for kids to watch the winged mammals as they go about their activities. Frogs are very popular here: The "Toadally Frogs" exhibit tells you all you would ever want to know about these colorful creatures.

Mbuna, the African name for the beautiful and varied cichlids fish, swim in the pools in the Africa Rainforest, while overhead tower some of the valuable trees we use for furniture, like the mahogany tree. From the Asian forests come bananas, and those of the Americas yield chocolate, avocado, and pineapple. Four 40-foot tall *Ficus benjamina* (Java laurel) trees form the core of the exhibit. Under the guidance of our Aggie entomologists, biological methods control insects in the rainforest; no toxic substances are used here.

You can get your food to go at the café or eat in the Garden Restaurant. The gift shop has it all: natural cosmetics, T-shirts, bugs, mugs, books, and cards, all beautifully crafted. Of course, you won't want to miss the other attractions here at Moody Gardens: the Aquarium Pyramid, the Discovery Pyramid, and an IMAX theater. And if you're too tired to go home, you can spend the night at the hotel here.

Tom's Thumb Nursery and Landscaping
Tom's thumb is definitely a green one.

Address: 2014 Forty-fifth Street, Galveston TX 77550

Phone: 409-763-4713

Website: www.Galveston.com/tomsthumb

Hours of operation: Monday–Saturday 9:00 A.M.–6:00 P.M., Sunday 10:00 A.M.–4:00 P.M.

Directions: I-45 south to Galveston. Continue on Broadway to Forty-fifth Street, and turn right. Nursery is on left at Forty-fifth and Avenue O.
Map Location: SES-Galveston

You hardly know where to look first at Tom's Thumb: Your eyes jump from one whimsical piece to another. Over here is a chair shaped like a fish. Over there, Tiki figures mark the entrance. Colorful Mexican frog planters and garden statuary could be just the thing to accent a light-hearted garden, while the many nautical objects vie for your attention, too. Scattered throughout are beautifully painted Adirondack chairs that could tempt you to sit awhile in your own garden.

Even in the layout of the grounds, you can see the hand of the landscaper, who has grouped the nursery stock to show it to advantage. Plants are arranged in a three-tiered design, which not only displays them attractively but also makes it easier to select just the plant you want. This results in a more intimate setting than that of many large nurseries.

Pathways meander invitingly here and there though the garden offerings. Whenever you think you have seen it all, another path beckons and entices you onward to new discoveries. You will see many varieties of trees and shrubs, perennials and annuals, all suited to the coastal areas. Since this is Galveston, there is a huge selection of palm trees and oleanders for a tropical seaside look in your garden.

A lovely gazebo area housing shade-loving plants and fountains is a quiet refuge from the blazing heat of a summer's day and will convince you that perhaps this kind of setting, plus a tall glass of iced tea, is the way to survive summertime.

Christmas is an especially festive time here. Add a playful touch to your holiday décor with a life-sized plastic palm tree glittering with tiny lights. Of course, the nursery offers many more traditional decorations, too, including sea-themed ones that are perfect for a Galveston beach house. You need look no farther than here for a custom wreath for your front door or mantel or for poinsettias to deck the halls with red and white.

North and West of Houston

What's the perfect antidote to a pressure-cooker workweek in Houston? Hop into the car, and take an easy drive out to the green rolling hills and small friendly towns in the countryside. The area west and north of Houston is a favorite weekend getaway destination for everyone, and especially for gardeners. Texans love the wide-open spaces; they counteract the close confines of city living. This area has everything you need for a total change of pace. Whether you are interested in gardens or wonderful specialized nurseries, history, the great outdoors, antiques, celebrations, or just a quiet weekend at a charming inn, all of that is here.

You can feel your blood pressure dropping as you pass bucolic scenes right out of a Grandma Moses painting: cows scattered across the lush pastures, fields of corn and other ripening crops, historical sites that tempt you to stop for a while, and everywhere you travel, a more laid-back approach to enjoying life.

Near to Houston is a large concentration of Christmas tree farms and pick-it-yourself sources of fresh fruits and vegetables. If you really want to get into the holiday spirit, a day spent in the fresh air cutting down your own tree will do the trick. In spring and summer, the many nearby farms invite you to harvest exactly the fruits or vegetables that you desire.

Drive west out of Houston on U.S. Highway 290 to Hempstead, where Peckerwood Garden is located. This outstanding collection is dedicated to the preservation of rare and unique dry-climate plants of the southwest American and Mexican desert area. Many of these plants can be purchased next door at Yucca Do Nursery. Hempstead also considers itself the watermelon capital of the world, so stop in at Di Iorio's, thump a few, and decide for yourself. The acres of concrete garden ornaments at Frazier's are sure to stock the perfect addition to your landscape.

Past Hempstead lies the town of Chappell Hill. Founded in 1847, the town boasts a charming main street, designated as a National Historic District, with carefully restored homes and shops. One of Chappell Hill's claims to fame is the Bluebonnet Festival held in early to mid-April. The fields surrounding the town are blanketed with indigo bluebonnets, and people gather to celebrate the state flower. Visitors can enjoy music, booths chock full of gardening and craft items, and tasty dishes to stave off hunger pangs as you take in the sights. Another blue flower, fragrant lavender, is abundant in all its forms at the Chappell Hill Lavender Farm.

Driving westward will bring you to Brenham, the hallowed home of Blue Bell ice cream. You can indulge in this icy treat at a tour of the Blue Bell Creameries, but there is more to Brenham than just the best ice cream this side of Italy.

As in Chappell Hill, Main Street in Brenham is a National Historic District, which means that the past has been preserved for our enjoyment in the present. Downtown is a relative term; small towns like Brenham are heavy on charm and light on hustle and bustle. Early settlers to the area crafted durable and delightful antiques, available in Brenham's many shops, as well as in Round Top and other nearby towns.

Brenham is at the heart of many winding roads of the celebrated Bluebonnet Trail. With their peak bloom in April, the bluebonnets, orange Indian paintbrush, and other native wildflowers fill the roadsides and fields with color. Turn off onto the less-traveled byways for uncrowded views of this seasonal glory. In addition to the Bluebonnet Trail, be sure to catch the Poinsettia Celebration at Ellison's. Nearby, the Antique Rose Emporium will be a highlight of your visit to Brenham since the store carries literally hundreds of antique roses.

Mention Round Top to gardeners, and they will begin to talk enthusiastically about the McAshan Herb Gardens at Festival Hill, created by Madalene Hill and Gwen Barclay. In addition to the huge collection of herbs to see, there are herbal forums that introduce you to these fascinating plants.

Round Top is world famous for the International Festival Institute at Festival Hill and the Round Top Antiques Fair. The International Festival Institute has grown since its founding in 1971 by concert pianist James Dick. The heart of the institute is the six-week summer music festival, which attracts internationally renowned musicians, but other concerts and workshops are also held throughout the year.

Dealers and collectors from near and far converge here for the biannual Round Top Antiques Fair, held in the fall and spring.

Knowledgeable collectors, who value these reminders of our heritage, quickly snap up the best of American country antiques from throughout the States.

Can't get to London to see Shakespeare at the Globe Theatre? Down the road from Round Top, the Shakespeare at Winedale program brings the bard's plays to life in a nineteenth-century barn at the University of Texas–Winedale Historical Center. A visit here is an enchanting way to enjoy Shakespeare, with melodious English phrases filling the air in the peace of a country setting.

Continuing a bit north and west, you come to Navasota, home of a great destination nursery with the amusing name of Martha's Bloomers. It features a café where you can refresh yourself with a delicious light lunch.

Then onward you travel to the mother lode of agricultural knowledge hereabouts, Texas A&M University. Its tremendous horticultural outreach to the community includes two main garden areas, the horticultural gardens and the holistic gardens. Visit them both—not only are they delightful oases, but they are also packed with information about and ideas for your own gardens.

For a refreshing change of pace, go jump in a lake: Lake Somerville. The catfish are leaping and biting, scenic hiking and biking trails beckon you, and campgrounds provide a place to pitch your tent. Did I mention horseback riding, swimming, bird watching, wildlife viewing, or any of the many other outdoor activities here?

Remnants of the early days of the Republic of Texas are abundant throughout the area, including the John P. Coles house in Independence. But Washington-on-the-Brazos is the lodestone for those curious about the story of Texas's struggle for independence.

Imagine yourself back in the early days of Texas as you stroll the trails, viewing the informative outdoor exhibits. Indoors, the Star of the Republic Museum expands on the theme of Texas independence with interactive displays. Finally, the Barrington Living History Farm gives visitors a glimpse into farm life of the 1850s, when Texas was young. Guides dressed in period costumes perform tasks that would have been necessary then, such as planting, cooking, and managing livestock. Visitors are encouraged to learn by doing, whether cooking over a fire, feeding the cows, or spinning cloth.

An afternoon visit to the miniature horse farm at the Monastery of Saint Clare, located northeast of Brenham, is a must. The adorable, fully grown small horses will charm children and adults alike and are gentle enough to be petted by the little ones. Handmade ceramics and other craft items are available at the gift shop.

When all the sightseeing is done, you will need somewhere to lay your weary head. Indulge yourself at a charming Victorian bed and breakfast, with all the comforts of home and then some. Let the musical sound of crickets outside a cozy farmhouse lull you to sleep while you are snug under a quilt. If you decide to camp out, find out why we say the stars at night are big and bright here in Texas. There are plenty of choices at all price levels.

Dining out can range from a quick pick-me-up to restaurants that feature the best international dishes. You can start your day with a leisurely breakfast in a country café, where you can mix with the locals and sample some real home cooking. At lunchtime, nothing beats Texas barbecue with the fixin's at a neighborhood place, which are thick in this area. Dinner can be casual and homey or as elegant as you wish.

The sun slides down into the west, the cows amble toward the barn, and you reluctantly head back to the big city. But never fear. A little of that relaxing country attitude will accompany you home to sustain you throughout the week.

Antique Rose Emporium

Everything's coming up roses here—and they're gorgeous.

Address: 10000 Highway 50, Independence TX 77833
Phone: 800-441-0002
Website: www.antiqueroseemporium.com
Hours of operation: Monday–Saturday 9:00 A.M.–5:30 P.M., Sunday 11:30 A.M.–
   5:30 P.M.
Directions: From Brenham, go north on route 50 to the location.
Map Location: NWS-Brenham area

As you enter the grounds of the Antique Rose Emporium, the first thing you see is a lovely wooden church, which is the picturesque

setting for many a country wedding. What more could a bride want: a church, quaint gazebo, winding paths through the well-landscaped grounds—and roses, thousands of them.

If you consider the rose the queen of the garden, then surely this is where she holds court. Owner Michael Shoup has tried to rescue many of the roses from pioneer days that bloomed well with little or no fussing over. These Texas natives perform well in our gardens, have heavenly scents, and are available in a wide variety of shapes and colors. But there are also many antique roses, and reading a list of the ones available is like reading a history of this most beloved flower.

After seeing—and sniffing—the roses in the display gardens, you may want to buy them immediately, or you can order them online if you wish. Either way, you will have top-quality stock and a very knowledgeable staff to answer any questions about their care. The roses in the garden are well marked, so you can jot down the ones you can't live without.

Roses look even better when planted with flowering Texas native plants, as they are here. Lantanas, verbenas, many kinds of salvias, and showy "yellow bells" complement the roses, showing them off to their best advantage.

Several well-stocked gift shops dot the grounds. The interior of one is painted an old-fashioned gray-green with stenciling that sets off the merchandise beautifully. A log cabin named "The Corn Crib" houses gardening essentials such as pots, fertilizer, and tools.

A visit to the display gardens reveals other delights. Children will absolutely adore the Beatrix Potter garden, with sweet additions such as Mrs. Tiggywinkle's mailbox and little pot people in and among the plants. A small sign here tells you that the rabbits "had bread and milk and blackberries for supper," and a propped-up shovel informs you that "Old Mrs. Rabbit was a widow." Elsewhere in the garden, children can discover the Tin Man, made of tin cans, a hat that is a funnel, metal boots, and a face that is a watering can. A bottle tree stands ready to trap any evil spirits lurking around, though I can't imagine any in this Eden.

Bluebonnet Trail

Heart-stopping beauty is around every corner here in April.

Address: Washington County and west toward the Hill Country near Austin
Phone: 888-273-6426 for wildflower information
Website: www.brenhamtexas.com
Directions: Drive out Highway 290 west until you begin to see wildflowers.
Map Location: NWS-Brenham area

Nothing makes a Texan's heart beat faster than a deep blue-and-white blanket of bluebonnets spread out over a hill as far as the eye can see. Bluebonnets, technically known as *Lupinus texensis,* are members of the lupine family. The bluebonnet beat out the prickly pear cactus for state flower back in 1901, and we are all grateful for that. It would be *unimaginable* to plop the kiddies in a field of prickly pear for that springtime picture to send to the grandparents.

The word "trail" is a little misleading, as this is not a one-time event but rather an invitation to come to the Hill Country anytime during late March or April to feast your eyes on the carpets of blue spread out everywhere. To add to the charm, orange-red Indian paintbrush, deep pink winecups, buttercups, and black-eyed Susans sprinkle their colors among the bluebonnets. Interestingly, the ever-resourceful Aggies at Texas A&M have bred a maroon bluebonnet—but some of us still prefer the fields of blue.

Drive out Highway 290 west from Houston any day during April, and you will begin to see sprinkles of white-tipped bluebonnets dotting the shoulders of the highway as you approach Chappell Hill and Hempstead. Since it is central to the Washington County wildflower area, Brenham is a good destination town. Remember to stop for a tour of the Blue Bell Creameries, home of that divine ice cream and the happiest cow commercials ever.

Driving west on 290 toward Brenham, turn north on FM 1155 at Chappell Hill toward Washington-on-the-Brazos, where the Republic of Texas was born in 1836. Then come down Highway 105 toward Brenham. From Brenham, take Highway 50 north toward Independence, FM 390 southwest toward Burton, then Highway 290 east back to Houston. All along the way are scenic towns, plenty of antiques, other garden sites (covered elsewhere in this book), and beautiful scenery everywhere you look. Chappell Hill hosts the Official Bluebonnet Festival of Texas in mid-April, where your family can enjoy live music, food, and crafts in a beautiful setting.

A few cautions will make the trip enjoyable. Be sure to respect any "no trespassing" signs you see. Plenty of public land is available to serve as a backdrop for your photos. One person can scout for scenic stopping points while the other drives. Watch your small kiddies—they dart around so quickly that another driver might not see them. Admire the livestock from a safe distance; they might think your hand is a salt lick and take a bite. And finally, before you sit on the ground for that contest-winning photo, check for anthills.

Chappell Hill Lavender Farm
Lavender is therapy for the spirit.

Address: 2250 Dillard Road, Brenham TX 77833
Phone: 979-251-8114
Website: www.chappellhilllavender.com
Hours of operation: Farm and gift shop open March to October (Saturday 9:00 A.M.–5:00 P.M., Sunday 11:00 A.M.–5:00 P.M.); other times, call for appointment
Directions: U.S. 290 toward Hempstead. After passing Hempstead, go 12 miles farther to Chappell Hill. Turn right at light onto FM 1155 going north. Travel 1.3 miles to Dillard Road and turn left; farm is on the right.
Map Location: NWS-Brenham area

According to *Culpeper's Complete Herbal,* written in the seventeenth century, lavender was pretty much a cure-all. Nowadays we focus more on its aromatic and culinary qualities, both of which are in evidence at Chappell Hill Herb Farms in Brenham. You can lose yourself in the fields of sweetly scented purple blooms and easily imagine that you might be in the fragrant heart of Provence.

Leaving the big city of Houston for the peaceful quiet of Brenham, Jim and Debbie McDowell found their vocation in growing lavender. It was a match made in heaven; the lavender flourished, and we can all now enjoy a jaunt to the country to cut the fragrant spikes of this plant, as well as to purchase products made from this beloved herb.

The Lavender Fest, usually held in late July, is a celebration featuring music and entertainment, craft items, and food, some of which incorporates lavender.

The cutting season usually lasts from mid- to late August. During that time you can walk the rows of plants and cut long stems to make lavender wands, an old-world craft. Or you can just gather a huge bunch and plop it into one of the attractive handmade pottery pieces sold here. With more than three thousand plants growing, there is more than enough for everyone.

If you would rather let someone else do the work, you can buy lavender or its many delightful products in the gift shop, where everything from luxurious bath products to note cards adorned with lavender is available. Surround yourself with this crisp clean scent in bath soaps, body lotions, and shower gels. To ensure sweet dreams, lightly mist your bed linens with a lavender spray, and burn a lavender candle, which will diffuse the scent into your room.

Provençal lavender is the preferred variety for cooking since it is a bit less assertive than the Spanish variety. Heavenly teas, coffees, and lemonades are available to take home. Be adventurous—try some lavender in salad dressings on a summer fruit salad or add it with other herbs to a marinade for grilled meats. Lavender really is an agreeable addition to many dishes.

Lavender, along with rosemary, is one of the most beloved herbs. Do yourself a favor and visit Chappell Hill Herb Farm to discover its many delights.

Di Iorio Farms and Roadside Market
Something for everyone, two-legged or four-legged

Address: Business 290, Hempstead TX 77445

Phone: 800-460-2688

Website: www.diioriofarms.com

Hours of operation: Daily 8:00 A.M.–7:00 P.M.

Directions: SH 290 west to Hempstead, exit Brookshire (FM 529); left at stop sign, go over the overpass, right at traffic light (Business 290); come into Hempstead over the hill; market is on right.

Map Location: NWS-Hempstead

When you are spending the weekend at the farm and want to do some down-home country cooking, head to Di Iorio's for that just-picked flavor. Chances are, those zucchini or peppers are fresh off the vine. Local produce in season is available, from Fredericksburg peaches to garden tomatoes. If your dining companion says, "Peas, please," there is an unusually good selection of fresh peas: purple hull, lady, and cream peas right out of the pea patch. You can whip up a gourmet feast or country barbecue with fresh veggies and fruits.

Speaking of vines, Hempstead bills itself as the watermelon capital of at least Texas—and maybe the world. Di Iorio's features a huge selection, so when those fruits that practically shout "It's summertime!" are ready in July, you will have lots to choose from, all thumping good.

Tasty country-fresh jams and jellies for your breakfast toast, local Hempstead honey, and a huge selection of nuts round out the available treats. If your pecan trees have dropped more nuts than you know what to do with, bring them along because they can be cracked and shelled while you shop.

However, veggies aren't everything that's here. Need a barbecue grill to cook some steaks? Di Iorio's offers a good selection. Want to take the load off your feet while the steaks cook? Check out their outdoor furniture, too. And, if looking at all those grills makes you think of burgers and such, there's a food-service area where you can get an order and wash it down with tangy lemonade.

Finding just the right objet d'art for the ranch house or garden is no problem. The feathered friends in your yard will appreciate a birdhouse with a roof made of Texas license plates, so they know they live in the Lone Star State. Tasty jams and sauces can add spark to your meals. If you are invited to a neighbor's for dinner, nip in here for a pretty plant to take along; Di Iorio's is also a full-service florist.

Need seeds or feed for Dobbin and the other farm critters? Your barnyard buddies can have a good selection of eats such as hen scratch and steamed crimped oats to nibble on. This is hardly your basic Purina chow; it's gourmet dining.

Frazier's Ornamental and Architectural Concrete, Inc.

Come for concrete, in all its appealing forms.

Address: 23200 Highway 6, Hempstead TX 77445
Phone: 979-921-2906
Website: www.fraziersconcrete.com
Hours of operation: Daily 9:00 A.M.–6:00 P.M., but closed Wednesday
Directions: SH 290 west toward Hempstead
Map Location: NWS-Hempstead

Who would imagine that concrete could be made up into creatively decorative pieces? In business for more than fifty years, Frazier's has become known for having just the right accent piece you crave. The retail shop is at this new location; the fabrication site is at the old location.

Ten acres is probably room enough to hold a wide variety of concrete garden art. As you walk, you will see many familiar farmyard creatures, as well as those who live only in imagination, such as griffons. A group of dog statues looks attentive, as though they were listening to a dog whisperer. Nearby, a group of concrete fire hydrants awaits the dogs: Someone has a sense of humor. A bright red boar (or maybe a razorback hog) seems to run by at full gallop, while life-sized pigs smile at you.

If your tastes run to art on a large scale, you might try a life-sized bronze horse or a four-foot-tall hand to beckon you into the garden. They even have a bas-relief of King Hammurabi, who wrote a code of laws for his subjects in Mesopotamia, now Iraq.

Not only can you look up at concrete castings, but you can also step on them. A unique set of stones has very detailed coins engraved on them: pennies, nickels, dimes, and quarters. You can scatter stones inscribed with log cabins, covered bridges, fossils, or oil wells throughout your garden.

More and more concrete summons you; this is surely concrete heaven. Birdbaths, planters, fountains, and even furniture are all made of concrete. Some are stained in different finishes, but most are the familiar soft gray-white. For those who love oriental garden décor, Frazier's offers a wide selection of Japanese design elements, including Buddhas. The Chinese goddess of serenity, Yan Ling, would impart a calming note to any garden.

You can also buy anything a well-stocked garden shop carries, including pots, hummingbird feeders, wall hangings, and pond supplies. But concrete is the main draw here, and nowhere is there a better selection.

Martha's Bloomers
Clever name, great garden store

Address: 8101 Highway 6, Navasota TX 77868
Phone: 936-870-4111
Website: www.marthasbloomers.com
Hours of operation: Monday–Saturday 9:00 A.M.–6:00 P.M., Sunday 11:00 A.M.–5:00 P.M.
Directions: US 290 west to SH 6 at Hempstead, turn north onto SH 6. Go to Navasota; the nursery is at the SH 6 bypass.
Map Location: NWS-Navasota

Martha's Bloomers advertises itself as "a garden store." That's like Tiffany's saying it sells jewelry. Oh, but what jewelry, and what a garden store! You can buy not only plants, decorative items, and garden art but also the antique cupboard displaying those objects if you cannot live without it.

As you approach, prize-winning garden displays in front tell you that this nursery devotes a great deal of attention to the plants it sells and is concerned about how to make them shine in your garden. Feel free to borrow their display ideas; they're outstanding.

Then, into the gift shop. Martha's Bloomers has its own line of botanical cosmetics, all of which have soft, fresh fragrances. A colorful table of tin spatter ware catches your eye; these bowls and pitchers give a country feel to any décor. Good decorating ideas abound: Lush vines twine around a mirror, and little garden and house ornaments add a whimsical touch.

By this time, you might be feeling a bit hungry. Time to take a needed break at Café M. Bloomers, where you will be seated in a cheery yellow room or on the vine-festooned patio. A complimentary demitasse of herb tea and some delicious slices of fruit and nut bread will refresh you while you contemplate the lunch menu.

Revived, you will set out to see the plants, which number a gazillion or so. If wet spots in your yard are a problem, let a bog garden inspire you. And if you would prefer to decrease your water bill, a xeriscaped garden will show you how to do so. Shining orange koi weave in and out of the plants in the attractive pond displays. Provençal-blue wagon wheels add a touch of color here and there amid the greenery on display. Venture inside the little cabin, which is full of pots of all kinds for sale.

Plants are babied at Martha's Bloomers. Trees in long rows are each tied to scaffolding posts like grapevines, an idea that keeps them from toppling over in strong winds.

Learn a little or a lot at the informative Saturday morning lectures in the spring. They're free and cover a range of timely topics. And you can improve your culinary expertise at one of the cooking classes; check the website, or call for reservations.

McAshan Herb Gardens at Festival Hill
Truly a garden of fragrant delights

Address: SH 237 at Jaster Road, Round Top TX 78954
Phone: 979-249-3129
Website: www.festivalhill.org
Hours of operation: No set hours; you can wander through the gardens
    whenever you like.
Directions: West on US 290 toward Austin, past Brenham. Turn south on SH
    237. Festival Hill is at Jaster Road and SH 237. Sign will say Menke House;
    gardens are behind house.
Map Location: WSA-Round Top

If your idea of heaven is peace, quiet, and fragrance and beauty all around, then this surely is heaven, here in the herbal gardens at Festival Hill. These beautiful grounds are a labor of love created by Madalene Hill and Gwen Barclay, her daughter. Those of you who have lived in Houston for a while may remember the outstanding meals at Hilltop Herb Farm, where the two were known for their imaginative uses of fragrant culinary herbs. Both women, who co-authored the bible for herb growing in our climate, *Southern Herb Growing,* are nationally known authorities on herbs in general, as well as the many uses of these plants, including culinary ones. The two women have been at Festival Hill since 1993, planning and nurturing these gardens and publicizing events such as herb semi-

nars, which introduce people to the delights and folklore of these plants.

As you walk around the grounds, you would be forgiven for thinking you were in an ancient herb garden in Italy or Greece. The decorative limestone objects and architectural structures look as though they have been there for centuries. A statue of Mary has nasturtiums crawling toward it as though seeking its cooling shade. But it's the herbs that draw you.

Most fascinating, perhaps, is the Pharmacy Garden. Much of the world's population still obtains its medicines from herbal plants. For eons, people relied on specially trained members of their clan to treat the sick with extracts from plants, such as digitalis and salicylates, that are still used today. Herbal remedies were a part of everyday life; a cup of chamomile tea was relaxing, and dill water is still used in Britain today to soothe babies' colic.

A serene and fragrant oasis is the Mediterranean Garden. Here, lavenders, santolinas, and various oreganos are laid out to show their cultural requirements. If a visit to Asia, India, South America, or Australia is not on your agenda, you can still experience their herbal bounty in various gardens devoted to these regions of the world.

The Sun/Shade Garden shows what will grow under those two conditions; no guesswork is required, so take good notes. Plants used for centuries in arid areas are found in the Medicinal Cacti Garden.

Butterflies who flit into these gardens must think this is paradise. Salvias and other flowering plants bloom abundantly, filling the air with fragrance and color. Humans often feel the same way as the butterflies. Something very primal happens in our brains when we brush a rosemary bush or rose and inhale the fragrance. Herbs have that effect on us.

𝒓

Peckerwood Garden
A gift for all of us—and well worth a visit

Address: 20571 FM 359 Road, Hempstead TX 77445

Phone: 979-826-3232

Website:www.peckerwoodgarden.com

Hours of operation: Saturday and Sunday, 1:00 P.M. to 4:00 P.M. on open days only, which are weekends in April, May, and October; check website for dates.

Admission: A $10.00 donation is required. Small children, baby strollers, and
pets are not allowed due to delicate or sharp plants they might encounter.
Directions: Highway 290 west toward Hempstead. Before Hempstead, turn
south on FM 359. Peckerwood Garden is just south of FM 359 and the
Business 290 intersection, on the right, next to Yucca Do Nursery.
Map Location: WSA-Hempstead area

For John Fairey, Peckerwood Garden began as—and continues to
be—a labor of love. Several years ago he and fellow plant enthusiast Carl Schoenfeld were invited by native plant expert Lynn Lowrey
to join a botanizing trip to northern Mexico. This led to an insa-
tiable quest by John Fairey to learn more about the fragile ecosystems that straddle the border of our two countries and to preserve
these rare species. Thanks to his dedication, we are able to visit a
magical collection of rare, beautiful, and irreplaceable plants, which
has been recognized by the National Garden Conservancy. Over the
years he has expanded his efforts to include propagation and seed-
sharing programs, so that everyone will be able to enjoy these extraordinary plants for years to come.

The area is divided into several very different gardens. First, a
wide sweep of open, sunny space hosts many diverse trees native to
northern Mexico and south Texas. Several trees in one small group
have been twined together to form a living sculpture.

You will then find your way to the woodland and perennial gardens. Paths wind through the dappled sunlit woods, inviting you to
admire the many lush gingers leaning languidly near the paths.
Glossy-leaved camellias add their tropical look, and soft-needled
yew trees add texture. Unusual variegated taros that look as though
Monet had splashed them with hues of green, gold, and cream add
colorful touches along the trails. Sculpted pieces scattered here and
there impart a finished look to the garden.

Of particular interest is the dry bed garden, reached by a bridge
across the stream that divides it from the perennial garden. Cacti,
agaves, palms, yuccas, sagos, and sages demonstrate the beauty and
variety of arid-area plants. Some are huge, broadleaved mammoths,
some are graceful and feathery, and many have attractive flowers. As
you look at them, be thankful that they are being preserved for future generations to appreciate.

Nearer to the house is a very architectural-looking pool area

Day Trips

incorporating river rocks, pebbles, a terra cotta fountain, and silvery cacti. It is at once striking in its beauty and calming in its simplicity.

Poinsettia Celebration at Ellison's Greenhouses
An elegant way to celebrate the holiday season

Address: 2107 East Stone Street, Brenham TX 77833

Phone: 979-836-6011

Website: www.ellisonsgreenhouses.com

Hours of operation: Saturday and Sunday before Thanksgiving, 10:00 A.M.–4:00 P.M.

Admission: adults, $2.00; children, $1.00

Directions: SH 290 west from Houston to Brenham. Just before Brenham, take FM 577 north, which is Horton Street. Ellison's is on the left, at Stone Street.

Map Location: NWS-Brenham

Imagine a greenhouse filled to bursting with lush red, white, peppermint-candy-striped, and pink poinsettias. Some look as though they have been spattered with paint, and even apricot, yellow, and perhaps other newer shades are being developed. Who couldn't get into a holiday mood? Maybe this year's Christmas card photograph is waiting to be taken. After all, what could be more appealing than your little ones smiling with Santa in front of the Texas-sized poinsettia tree?

Poinsettias are hard to beat for instant holiday cheer. Their tropical look fits in well with our Gulf Coast winters, which are not exactly Currier-and-Ives snowscapes. Best of all, you can usually cut them back and retire them to your garden for the summer, and, with a little luck, they'll show their colors again next November.

Of course, you will want to buy some of these beauties. Greenhouse team members accompany you, answering questions and helping you to choose the perfect plants. Then they pack them up for the ride home to Houston. If you are pressed for time, there are booths already stocked with lush plants, so that you can choose, pay, and be on your way.

You can attend informative miniseminars during the celebration. Some of the country's top poinsettia breeders are present, getting your feedback about which flowers prove to be most popular with the public. Those poinsettia varieties are the ones you are apt to see more of in future years. So if you are a loyal Texas A&M fan, go buy a houseful of maroon poinsettias, and tell the breeders how much you love that color.

Still, this is a celebration of the poinsettia, so you and the children will have plenty of fun here, too. There are arts and crafts for all ages, so you can do a little last-minute holiday shopping—or start it. And note that the admission fee always benefits a local charitable organization.

Texas A&M University Horticultural and Holistic Gardens
The folks at A&M can show us all how it's done.

Horticultural Gardens

Address: Hensel Street, College Station TX 77843
Phone: 979-845-3658
Website: www.hortgardens.tamu.edu
Hours of operation: Daily, dawn to dusk, seven days a week
Directions: SH 290 from Houston toward Hempstead. At Hempstead, turn north onto SH 6. At College Station, bear to the left onto Business 6, which becomes Texas Avenue. Cross University Avenue, and the next left is Hensel. Go right when Hensel dead-ends, and you will see parking for the gardens.
Map Location: NWS-College Station

Holistic Garden

Address: West Campus, College Station TX 77843
Phone: 979-845-3915
Website: www.aggie-horticulture.tamu.edu/holisticgarden
Hours of operation: Daily, dawn to dusk, seven days a week
Directions: Follow previous directions to University Avenue, but turn left onto University. Turn left at Olsen Boulevard, which is on the West Campus. Follow Olson to parking lot 74. The gardens are just south of the Horticulture and Forest Sciences Building.
Map Location: NWS-College Station

Founded in 1876, Texas A&M University was the first public institution of higher learning in the state of Texas. What concerns us here is the agricultural mandate of A&M, which includes teaching, research, and extension (outreach to the community). The gardens at A&M fulfill all three functions admirably. Not surprisingly, the Aggie horticulture students meticulously care for both large gardens, learning as they do so.

The two gardens are the horticultural and the holistic gardens. The former focus on plants as a part of the landscape and contain more than twenty-five hundred specimens in thirty different areas. *Holistic* means defining the functional relationship between the parts and the whole, and this latter garden integrates awareness of the needs of the ecosystem with the requirements of gardeners, including those who might have a disability.

In the horticultural gardens, the plants are clearly labeled, and information sheets guide you through the one-eighth-mile walk along winding paths. Plaques at the entrance to each garden explain the garden's significance, whether it is a native habitat garden attractive to birds and butterflies or a found rose garden full of plants grown from cuttings of roses that might otherwise be lost. Glean decorative ideas from the sculptural additions dotting the landscape, as well as the dry streambeds and inventive use of limestone.

Texas' answer to the fluffy pink flowers of cherry trees is the lacy blooms of the crape myrtle. In the summer, visit the crape myrtle trail in the gardens for a gorgeous vista while you walk. The nursery and greenhouse are active research areas, and a sign entreats you to "keep gate closed—rabbits running amok." The mental image this evokes is amusing; obviously, the bunnies are busy but unwanted additions to the research staff.

A charming reproduction of a tiny nineteenth-century pioneer log cabin that housed a family of ten is the focal point of a garden filled with heirloom plants from that era. Early settlers quickly learned by trial and error which plants could cure various ailments, as well as which varieties of food plants grew best in this climate. And they did this without the benefit of the Internet.

Designed with persons with disabilities in mind, the holistic garden showcases many adaptations to special needs, such as extrawide paths and raised beds for easier access. Gardening tools are ingeniously designed to make garden tasks easier.

The
Garden Lover's
Guide to
Houston

This is a great destination for school children. Colorful interactive exhibits make learning about nature effortless and fun. Kids can dig for worms and also watch butterflies feed on fruits and nectar; activities like these will help them better understand the interdependence among all of earth's creatures.

Throughout the year, plant sales, a garden market, and a variety of short courses and informal lectures present the philosophy and actual products of the holistic garden to the community. Produce is grown using only organic techniques—the holistic approach at work.

Various subgardens include an orchard, kitchen garden, butterfly garden, discovery garden, enabling garden, wetland ecosystem, sensory garden, herb garden, and more. In homage to the talented Aggie horticulturists, there is even a maroon-and-white garden.

What could be better than visiting gardens that showcase good gardening practices and creative landscape design? The sun slants through the trees, and a cardinal's "what-cheer" fills the air. Sit for a moment, relax, and be inspired.

Yucca Do Nursery, Inc.
You don't need to travel to the wilds to buy rare plants.

Address: FM 359 and FM 3346, Hempstead TX 77445
Phone: 979-826-4580
Website: www.yuccado.com
Hours of operation: Friday to Sunday, 9:00 A.M.–5:00 P.M. on open days
    only, which are weekends in April, May, and October; check website
    for dates.
Directions: West on Hwy 290 from Houston, exit at FM 359, south for 2
    miles; nursery is on right.
Map Location: WSA-Hempstead area

Perhaps you have visited Peckerwood Garden next door and fallen in love with the distinctive flora native to the arid regions of the Southwest, but where can you buy them? Fortunately, a mere step or two over to Yucca Do Nursery will enable you to bring these treasures home.

Carl Schoenfeld, the owner of Yucca Do, has traveled to the back of beyond in his quest for unique plants that are showy, adaptable, and, most important, drought tolerant. Expeditions to the south-western part of the United States, Mexico, and more recently to Africa have yielded everything from small bulbs to large trees. All are carefully propagated and nurtured at Yucca Do so that gardeners can grow these specimens that otherwise might be lost to future generations.

These plants aren't prima donnas; they have been chosen for their toughness and ability to handle extremes of temperature and moisture. As the evidence for global warming grows, gardeners are wise to look for plants that need little water and those that adapt well to the area we live in.

Drought-tolerant gardening does not have to mean a garden full of cactus. Yucca Do stocks enough perennials, bulbs, bromeliads, cycads, ferns, trees, and grasses to create a varied, beautiful, and verdant garden that will be easy to maintain and enjoy.

Imagine a stately blue-gray agave as the centerpiece of a garden, surrounded by a drift of bluebonnets in the spring. A magnet for hummingbirds, the red bottlebrush becomes a striking focal point in the garden when surrounded by white delphiniums, purple bletilla, or rosy-pink cannas as the season progresses. Beauty and drought tolerance can go hand in hand.

The display gardens will give you even more options. Plants that attract butterflies, plants for a water feature, and vining plants are some of the variations on the drought-tolerant theme that will pique your interest. The subtle grays and beiges of a dry creek bed are strikingly contrasted by the shocking pink portulacas that overflow its banks.

Stroll around and take note of what appeals to you, asking questions if necessary; the staff is knowledgeable about their stock. Choose and then buy the plants you want, knowing that they will rest easy in your garden and give you years of pleasure.

Garden Clubs and Plant Societies

ardeners are like clusters of daffodils; they're sociable and like to be around others of their own kind. After all, if you are passionate about camellias, you want to learn everything you can about these luxuriant bloomers, so you would want to attend the meetings of a society that is focused solely on camellias. Even the ubiquitous daylily has several groups of devotees that meet, possibly to discuss propagation techniques that will produce even more striking cultivars than are available currently.

These societies usually have speakers at their meetings, sponsor plant sales, host field trips to gardens of interest, and generally serve to bring together people who share a common interest in a particular plant. For instance, what could be a better way to learn about the queen of the garden than to visit a garden where acres are devoted to the rose in all its glory? You can pick up valuable information about where and how to plant roses—or other flora—in your own garden.

While the various garden societies are usually dedicated to a particular plant, the common denominator that brings members of a garden club together is an interest in gardening. Yet these clubs provide so much more than meeting places for gardeners; most of them are very involved in the communities of which they are a part.

Clubs

Garden clubs fulfill this outreach function in various ways. They beautify their communities by planting and maintaining gardens, plazas, and esplanades. Like the specialized plant societies, the clubs educate their members by hosting speakers knowledgeable in all areas of horticulture. These clubs promote gardening in harmony with nature and conserve valuable heirloom plant materials for future generations.

Probably the best-known and largest garden club in our area is the venerable Garden Club of Houston, sponsor of the annual Bulb and Plant Mart held in the fall. However, many smaller garden clubs might be just right for you.

Garden Clubs

Alvin Garden Club (Alvin)
Blue Bend Garden Club
Blue Triangle Garden Club
Bluebonnet Garden Club
Bouquettes Garden Club
Brazosport Garden Club
Brightwater Garden Club
Cabildo Garden Club
Campus Garden Club
Champion Forest Garden Club
Columbus Garden Club
Clear Lake City Garden Club
Clear Lake Forest Garden Club
Community Garden Club (Santa Fe area)
Creative Gardeners (Pasadena)
Crestwood Garden Club
Dig 'n' Design Garden Club (Clear Lake)
Far Corners Garden Study Club
Fleetwood Garden Club
Flora Luncheon Study Club (Bay City)
Fondren Park Home and Garden Club
Forest Cove Garden Club
Forest Garden Club
Forest West Garden Club

Founders' Garden Club of Brazosport
Friendship Garden Club (Katy)
Frey Garden Club (Houston)
Galveston Garden Club
Garden Club of Houston
Garden Club of Pasadena
Garden Club of Sealy
Gardeners by the Bay
Gateway Ace Garden Club
Gulf Coast Gardeners
Gulf Coast Gardeners Forum
Gung Hoe Gardeners (Texas City)
Hearthstone Garden Club
Heritage Gardeners (Friendswood)
Houston Bonsai Society
Houston Cactus and Succulent Society
Houston Council of Garden Clubs
Houston Federation of Garden Clubs
Houston Rose Society
Houstonia Garden Club
Hunter's Creek Garden Club
Japanese Garden Society of Houston
Jersey Village Garden Club
Kemah–Bay Area Garden Club (League City)
Kingwood Garden Club
La Marque Garden Club
La Porte–Bayshore Garden Club
Lake Houston Gardeners
Lake Jackson Garden Club (Lake Jackson)
Lake Olympia Garden Club (Missouri City)
Lakeview Garden Club
Lakewood Forest Garden Club
Lazy Daisy Garden Club
League City Garden Club (League City)
Liberty Garden Club
Mangum Manor Home and Garden Club
Meadowbrook Garden Club
Memorial Northwest Ladybugs Garden Club (Spring)
Men's Garden Club of Houston

Meyerland Garden Club
Mums and More Garden Club
Nassau Bay Garden Club (Nassau Bay)
New Caney Garden Club
New Century Garden Club (Richmond)
Newport Garden Club (League City)
Norchester Garden Club
Nottingham Country Garden Club (Katy)
Nottingham Trail Gardeners
Panorama Garden Club
Park People
Parkview Estates Garden Club (Pasadena)
Pasadena Garden Club, Inc.
Pearland Garden Club
Petal Pushers Garden Club (Deer Park)
Petit Jardin Garden Club
Pine Village Garden Club
Piney Point Garden Club
Piney Woods Garden Club
Plant and Pray Garden Club
Quail Valley Garden Club Inc. (Missouri City)
River Oaks Garden Club
Salt Water Garden Club (Bayou Vista)
Southampton Garden Club
Sprig and Sprout Garden Club
Sugar Creek Garden Club (Sugar Land)
Sugar Land Garden Club
Sweeny Garden Club
Texas City Garden Club (Texas City)
Texas Star Garden Club
Tri-County Diggers Garden Club
Timbergrove Garden Club (Seabrook)
United Garden Club
Urban Harvest
Weed 'n' Wish Garden Club
Wilchester Garden Club
Windrose Garden Club
Woodlands Garden Club
Wooster Garden Club (Baytown)

The
Garden Lover's
Guide to
Houston

Plant Societies

African Violets

NASA Area African Violet Society
Meetings: Clear Lake Park building, 5001 NASA Road,
Seabrook TX 77586
Website: www.avsa.org

Spring Branch African Violet Club
Meetings: members' homes
Phone: 281-358-3298
Website: www.orgsites.com/tx/sbavs.index

Amaryllis

Houston Amaryllis Society
Meetings: Houston Garden Center, Hermann Park
Phone: 713-284-1986

Begonias

ABS/Astro Branch
Meetings: Houston Garden Center, Hermann Park
Phone: 713-284-1986
Website: http://absastro.tripod.com/branch.htm

ABS/Houston Satellite Branch
Meetings: Amegy, League City, TX
Phone: 409-927-8638

ABS/San Jacinto Branch
Meetings: Community room of Pasadena Town Square Shop-
ping Mall, Pasadena, TX
Phone: 713-941-7158

Bonsai

Houston Bonsai Society
Meetings: Houston Garden Center, Hermann Park
Phone: 713-284-1986
Website: www.houstonbonsai.com

Bromeliads

Bromeliad Society of Houston
Meetings: Houston Garden Center, Hermann Park
Website: www.bromeliadsocietyhouston.org

Cactus

Houston Cactus and Succulent Society
Meetings: Houston Garden Center, Hermann Park
Website: www.hcsstex.org

Camellias

Houston Camellia Society
Meetings: Check website
Website: www.camellia.gulfcoast-gardening.com/clublist.htm

Chrysanthemums

Greater Houston Chrysanthemum Society
Meetings: Houston Garden Center, Hermann Park
Phone: 713-284-1986
Website: www.mums.org/chapters/tx.htm

Daylilies

Brazosport Daylily Society
Meetings: Lake Jackson library
Phone: 979-297-1271
Website: www.daylilies.org/AHSreg6.html

Cypress Creek Daylily Club
Meetings: Mercer Arboretum
Website: www.daylilies.org/AHSreg6.html

Houston Area Daylily Society
Meetings: Houston Garden Center, Hermann Park
Phone: 713-284-1986

Houston Hemerocallis Society
Meetings: Houston Garden Center, Hermann Park
Phone: 713-284-1986

Lone Star Daylily Society
Meetings: Alvin Senior Citizens Building, Alvin, TX
Phone: 281-388-4298

Ferns

Texas Gulf Coast Fern Society
Meetings: Houston Garden Center, Hermann Park
Phone: 713-284-1986
Website: www.tgcfernsoc.org

Fruits

Gulf Coast Fruit Study Group
Meetings: 3033 Bear Creek Drive, Houston TX 77084
Phone: 281-855-5600
Website: http://harris-tx.tamu.edu/hort/fruit.htm

Herbs

South Texas Unit of the Herb Society of America
Meetings: Houston Garden Center, Hermann Park
Phone: 713-513-7808
Website: www.herbsociety-stu.org

Pioneer Unit of the Herb Society of America
Meetings: Check website
Website: www.herbsociety.org/cms_unit_list.php

Hibiscus

Lone Star Chapter of the American Hibiscus Society
Meetings: Houston Garden Center, Hermann Park
Website: www.lonestarahs.org

Space City Chapter of the American Hibiscus Society
Meetings: Harris County Activity Center, 7340 Spencer,
   Pasadena
Website: www.spacecityahs.org

Native Plants

Native Plant Society of Texas
Meetings: Houston Arboretum and Nature Center
Website: www.npsot.org/houston

Oleanders

International Oleander Society
Meetings: Check website
Website: www.oleander.org

Orchids

Galveston Orchid Society
Meetings: Nessler Center, Texas City
Website: www.galvestonorchidsociety.org

Houston Orchid Society
Meetings: Houston Garden Center, Hermann Park
Website: www.houstonorchidsociety.org

Palms

Houston Texas Area Chapter, International Palm Society
of America
Meetings: Check website
Website: www.palms.org/houston

Plumerias

Plumeria Society of America
Meetings: Houston Garden Center, Hermann Park
Website: www.theplumeriasociety.org

Roses

Houston Rose Society
Meetings: Houston Garden Center, Hermann Park
Website: www.houstonrose.org

Texas Rose Rustlers
Meetings: Check website
Website: www.texasroserustlers.org

Volunteer Opportunities

re you looking for garden-related ways to give something back to your community? Does working outside in the sunshine while being serenaded by birdsong appeal to you? Or how about helping children reap the bounty of fresh-picked veggies they have grown themselves? These and more opportunities abound with the Master Gardener programs in the greater Houston area. In addition, numerous other organizations would be grateful for your help.

However, you do not need to be a Master Gardener to dig in the dirt; parks and gardens all over the area would welcome an extra pair of hands to beautify our city. Several organizations host plant sales and could use your assistance. A bonus is that you get to check out the offerings before the sale and perhaps even buy a favorite new plant.

You might visit the Cockrell Butterfly Center or Moody Gardens and become so entranced with their programs that you want to share your enthusiasm with the public. Become a tour guide, and show everyone both young and old the wonders that attracted you. Children are receptive audiences because they are so curious about the world they live in. Whether you are showing them a butterfly chrysalis or a huge vine in the rainforest, their sense of wonder and delight will repay your efforts many times over.

If you love to hear the sound of your own voice, there are garden-related speakers' bureaus that will welcome your expertise and passion for a subject. This is a great way to meet new people and share your love of gardening with them.

As you can see, the possibilities are endless, as are the rewards. Nothing can equal the pleasure of knowing that you have given something of yourself to another without any other recompense than the satisfaction of a job well done. You will be a better person for it, and the community benefits, too. It's a win-win situation for everyone.

Texas Cooperative Extension Master Gardener Program

The best way to combine gardening with volunteering is to become a Master Gardener. The Master Gardener Program operates in conjunction with the Texas Cooperative Extension, which is in turn affiliated with Texas A&M University.

The Master Gardeners are trained volunteers who share their gardening expertise with the communities in which they live. Master Gardeners complete a course of study covering a variety of topics relating to all phases of gardening. Some of the most talented horticultural and agricultural experts from Texas A&M and other sources lecture on their specialties. After the Master Gardener interns pass an exam and are certified, they then perform a number of hours of volunteer service. There is a volunteer activity to suit everyone, no matter where your interests lie.

Some of the required hours are spent answering phoned-in questions from the public. Phone duty represents a great learning opportunity for the volunteers, too, since they must occasionally research difficult questions. In addition to phone duty, volunteers still have plenty of chances to get their hands dirty, to watch a tiny seedling mature into a bush laden with peppers, and to revel in the heady scent of a rose they're pruning.

In addition to working at the Extension offices, Master Gardeners are encouraged to reach out to the community. One way to help is to be involved in school gardening projects. The School Cylinder

Gardening Program is a terrific way for children to learn that gardening can be fun and that the fruits—or veggies—of their labors are tasty, too. The children are proud of their accomplishments and often get their families involved; thus everyone eats a healthier diet.

All of the counties in the Houston area have Master Gardener classes available at various locations. These begin at different times of the year, and both daytime and evening courses are available, so you should be able to find one that is convenient for your schedule. Here are a few phone numbers to call if you are interested. You can also check the website, http://harris-tx.tamu.edu/hort/mastergardener.htm, for more information.

Fort Bend County Master Gardeners

Classes meet at the Fort Bend County Extension Office, 1402 Band Road, Rosenberg TX 77471. The phone number is 281-341-7068.

Harris County Master Gardeners

Classes meet at the Harris County Extension Office, 3033 Bear Creek Drive, Houston TX 77084. The phone number is 281-855-5600. Additional classes meet at the following location:

Harris County Precinct 2, 1202 Genoa Red Bluff Road, Houston TX 77034. The phone number is 281-991-8437.

Galveston County Master Gardeners

Galveston County Extension Office, 5115 Highway 3, Dickinson TX 77539. The phone number is 281-534-3413, extension 1.

Montgomery County Master Gardeners

Montgomery County Extension Office, 9020 FM 1484, Conroe TX 77303. The phone number is 936-539-7824.

Other Opportunities for Volunteering

Volunteer
Opportunities

One of the most active garden organizations in our area is Urban Harvest, which reaches out to the community in several ways. Gardeners can work in community gardens that help feed those who are less fortunate by growing nutritious produce for them. Earth-friendly gardening is the focus of Urban Harvest's classes, which cover topics such as permaculture, different ways to start a community or school garden, and gardening basics for the novice. Their resources include a book library, a seed library for heirloom and unusual varieties, and members who are willing to help you with garden problems. They also sponsor the Bayou City Farmers Market (reviewed in the Farmers' Market chapter).

Leaf through this book: An abundance of opportunities exists for you to help at many of the venues listed, especially those in chapters 1–3 and chapter 6. Sprucing up a park or garden is an ongoing activity and an obvious way to help. You would be welcomed with open arms, most likely bearing rakes.

People are curious about a garden they are visiting, which is why they came in the first place. Imparting your specialized knowledge about that garden is your gift to them. Even though you are trained in how to give tours, you can still put some of your own personality into them and tell some of your own anecdotes to make the tour memorable; this is a great activity for the extrovert who loves to talk. The public gardens mentioned in chapter 1 would welcome your help.

An enjoyable time can be yours when you work at one of the many annual garden events in the area. As a single example, you could get involved in selling plants at the Mercer March Mart. Pick an event, and call to volunteer.

It is essential that our children grow up with a love of the natural world. What better way to introduce them to the wonders of nature than to volunteer at one of the parks or arboreta that have extensive programs for the young and the not so young? Kids are so enthusiastic about butterflies, flowers, snakes, and everything else in nature that it is hard for us not to get excited, too. Teaching, giving tours, and supervising hands-on workshops are some of the ways to help children enjoy gardening and nature-oriented activities they will remember for a lifetime.

These are but a few of the volunteer activities you can pursue. If your muse is a literary one, offer to write, edit, or distribute an organization's newsletter. Almost any group would welcome your computer skills.

Last, but certainly not least, one of the most rewarding activities is helping to maintain the gardens at the Ronald McDonald House near the Texas Medical Center. The peace and beauty of the garden here is balm to the soul of a parent whose child is hospitalized.

No matter how busy our lives are, garden lovers can volunteer in some capacity. Giving to others brings immense satisfaction to the giver. Try it—you'll see.

Volunteer
Opportunities

Retail Sources

The answer to a gardener's prayer: If it is related to gardening, this chapter will tell you where to find it. Whether you are looking for a concrete squirrel, painting of the same, food for the beastie, or a book that tells how to outwit squirrels, it's all here.

Thanks to our relatively benign growing climate, nurseries all over the area are as plentiful as azalea blooms in springtime. Some of them carry a little bit of everything, while others specialize in certain types of plants. African violets, bonsai, tropicals, roses, orchids, or cactus all have specialty nurseries or shops devoted to them. If orchids are your passion, for instance, you will probably encounter a wider selection and more pertinent advice at a specialty shop. On the other hand, if you just need several flats of pansies or begonias, it might be easier to patronize a neighborhood nursery or one of the meganurseries.

A very important subset of nurseries is composed of those that feature Texas native plants. The trees and shrubs can form the backbone of your garden, while vines and flowers can add color, fragrance, and texture to the landscape. Once established, native plants usually need little water or care; after all, they are from around here, so they settle in nicely.

Other nurseries highlight organically raised plants. We are but one species on the planet, and we should learn to coexist with the other inhabitants. An organic garden is usually healthier, flowers more abundantly, and attracts birds and butterflies for our enjoyment and their sustenance. Everyone wins.

There is more to a garden than greenery, however. Water features, sculpture, and antiques add an extra touch that personalizes your space. Several businesses specialize in these décor items. The cooling splash of a fountain will soothe all who hear it, while a concrete canine snoozing among the petunias will delight you. A well-placed sculptural accent may be just the thing to highlight a garden bed.

A vibrant pink azalea or another plant is a welcome gift for anyone, gardener or not. Nursery gift shops also stock a good selection of gardening books, many targeted to our area. Be stylishly protected from the elements in gardening clothes, and pick up some garden-related items for your children, too. It's all here and more.

Adkins Architectural Antiques and Treasures

Perfect accent pieces for your English country garden in Texas

Address: 3515 Fannin Street, Houston TX 77004
Phone: 713-522-6547
Website: www.adkinsantiques.com
Hours of operation: Monday–Saturday 9:30 A.M.–5:30 P.M., Sunday noon–
    5:00 P.M.
Directions: On Fannin at Berry; two blocks north of Alabama
Map Location: W1

Do not let the name mislead you: The indoor antiques are only a part of Adkins's inventory. They carry a large stock of antique treasures for the garden that will look like they have been there forever. Obviously, everything outside is weatherproof and will last for eons, even in our capricious climate.

While you relax on an antique wrought iron bench with a dolphin motif, you can watch the kiddies climb over a life-sized longhorn. Choose from a variety of iron table-and-chair sets that would look great in a shady nook in the garden. More heavy metal: iron gates, slate-colored urns on pedestals, wall plaques, and planters abound.

Winsome iron rabbits peek out from under the greenery, while iron chickens and roosters scattered around a garden would add a rustic touch. And here is proof positive that pigs do indeed fly; you can buy one or a herd of angelic winged little porkers to prove it.

The star motif is alive and well here, ranging from small ones that could enhance a fence post, up to giant five-foot ones that would make a statement adorning the front façade of a warm-toned lime-stone ranch house in the country. Continuing the ranch theme, an aged dinner bell adorned with a cow or other animal would be a great way to call the kids home.

There's more: gliders and metal porch chairs, like the ones you remember from Grandma's house, French baker's racks, and old tractor seats, which can be spruced up with a coat of shiny-red lacquer and made into unusual seating.

If you are in the market for those old architectural pieces that can personalize your garden, look no further: A set of Moorish window grates that looks straight out of the *Arabian Nights* awaits you. Marble pieces can be used to top an outdoor table that will stand up to the elements. An old claw-foot bathtub would add a period touch indoors but could also become an unusual planter or doggy splash tub.

There's a place for new furnishings and garden décor, but if you adore the mellow look of well-used antiques in your garden, this is the place to go.

All Seasons Nursery

Water, water everywhere—and scenic, too

Address: 4901 Vista, Pasadena TX 77506
Phone: 281-487-8733
Website: None listed
Hours of operation: Monday–Saturday 8:00 A.M.–6:00 P.M. (5:30 P.M. in winter), Sunday 9:00 A.M.–5:00 P.M. year-round
Directions: Sam Houston Parkway south to Pasadena, exit onto Vista, go almost to Preston.
Map Location: SE2

Retail Sources

You're in the *country* now. If you don't believe it, turn around and notice the hens and roosters that have been prancing along behind you, commenting on your choices.

Ponds and other water features are the specialty at All Seasons, and their goal is to achieve a scenically landscaped area that looks as though it occurred naturally and has been there forever.

Helena and Tini Geraldes, the owners, will guide you through the process even if you know nothing about water except that it's wet. They will handle everything from concept to finished waterscape, even stocking the pond with koi and water-loving plants.

For ideas, stroll around and view several examples of lush waterfalls spilling over very natural-looking rocks. Your ears catch the sound of a burbling creek in a secluded dell that looks as though it were in the middle of a dense forest. But no, you're still in sunny Pasadena. Another water feature is landscaped as a lush tropical rainforest; you half expect to see colorful parrots swooping down at any moment.

If your garden area is only the size of a small patio, you can still have the calming sound of a water feature. A tall cobalt blue glazed pot can be fitted for a fountain and would be an attractive complement to a mass of garden greenery and flowers.

For thousands of years, people of the hot desert areas of the world have realized the importance and soul-soothing qualities of listening to the trickling of water. The Alhambra fortress in Spain is filled with fountains, the sounds of which were considered necessary to the well-being of its inhabitants. We in Houston should take note and surround ourselves with these musical sounds when summer is at its merciless worst. Let the folks at All Seasons help you to start enjoying the cooling splash of a fountain or pond.

TIP Flowers will last longer if you recut the stems when you get them home, strip away all of the leaves that will be under water, change the water daily, and drop a penny into the water (the copper in the penny is a germicide).

Anderson Landscape and Nursery, Inc.

Go native here. You'll be glad you did.

Address: 2222 Pech Road, Houston TX 77055
Phone: 713-984-1342
Website: None listed
Hours of operation: Call first before going
Directions: North of Hammerly, east of Bingle
Map Location: W2A

Nowadays it's a good idea to stock your garden with native plants, which are usually well adapted to our area, less likely to be bothered by bugs, and grow enthusiastically. Texas natives make up a large portion of the plants for sale at Anderson Landscape and Nursery. Patsy Anderson, who owns the nursery with her husband, Mike, is the daughter of the famed horticulturist Lynn Lowrey, who advocated the use of native plants. Lowrey was responsible for introducing many natives to Houston landscapes and did much of the propagation here at Anderson Nursery. That tradition is alive and well today.

Butterflies fill the air, no doubt due to the many Mexican butterfly weed plants here and there. As you might know, this is a host plant for the monarch butterflies, and you would be doing them a favor by having one or more of these plants in your garden. Coral bean plants, with their tubular red flowers, are another surefire butterfly and hummingbird magnet.

Other attractive natives include the Texas mountain laurel, which is covered with purply-blue flowers that have the odor of Grape Kool-Aid—*really*. And the Fanick phlox, which is drought tolerant and blooms with lovely pink flowers all summer, will charm those of you who love this old-fashioned favorite.

Huge shade trees casting a cool shadow are underplanted with shade-loving plants so that you can easily visualize what would look good in your own shady garden.

You can always learn a lot from the information cards that are placed near the plants. And if you have further questions, just ask the staff, who will be glad to help you.

107

Retail Sources

There are many reasons to have a habitat garden that is easy on the eyes, the water meter, and the planet. You would do well to have the experts at Anderson plan the perfect garden that will give you many hours of enjoyment.

> **TIP** Grasses are beautiful accent plants, adding year-round structure and texture. Varying from ground covers to tall waving plumed plants, grasses range in color from blue gray through greens to burgundy. Just be sure to put them with other plants that have similar water requirements.

Another Place in Time

Charming, personal, and well thought out

Address: 1102 Tulane, Houston TX 77008
Phone: 713-864-9717
Website: www.anotherplaceintime.com
Hours of operation: Tuesday–Saturday 9:00 A.M.–6:00 P.M.; Monday 9:30 A.M.–5:30 P.M., Sunday 10:00 A.M.–5:00 P.M. year-round
Directions: North on Heights Boulevard to Eleventh Street, turn left on Eleventh. On corner of Eleventh and Tulane
Map Location: NW1

Another Place in Time promotes itself as "Your Uncommon Garden Center," and it certainly lives up to its billing; this is not a cookie-cutter nursery. A weathered iron arch flanked by bamboo shooting skyward beckons you to enter. Stepping along mulched pathways that feel soft underfoot, you look up and see wall hangings on the lattice dividers that complement the plants. No endlessly long tables to overwhelm you; the small plant tables here are easy to navigate. And you will appreciate the way gifts to enhance your garden are scattered throughout so as to spark your imagination. Information cards with the plants are helpful, particularly those for the native plants.

As you enter the tropical room, you will think you're on an island when you see the star-quality bromeliads and lush orchids. Take home some colorful bromeliads artfully arranged on driftwood. They will have a happy home and flourish in the warm humid air on a patio.

If you have questions about the care of bromeliads or anything else, the friendly assistants are ready to help with answers, particularly about their collection of rare and unusual varieties. For instance, a curly bird's nest fern, with its ruffled leaf edges, is a unique variation on the more usual bird's nest fern.

In the gift shop are some distinctive sculptural pieces, such as copper swirls that twirl gently in the breeze, in addition to much more metal work of all kinds. Bring the garden indoors with a piece of stained glass that has a garden theme. Whimsical tin-can sculptures of dogs and cats add a playful touch to your garden. Tall bookcases showcase garden books for our area, as well as colorful artistic additions to your indoor or outdoor décor. All in all, this is a charming place to while away some time and let your imagination have free rein.

Bill Bownds Nursery

Worth the country drive out here for a tree

Address: 10519 FM 1464, Richmond TX 77469
Phone: 281-277-2033
Website: None listed
Hours of operation: Monday–Saturday 9:00 A.M.–5:30 P.M.; closed Sunday
Directions: Highway 59 south to Bissonnet, west to Highway 6, turn left, and
    head south on Highway 6, then turn right on Old Richmond Road. Continue onto Boss Gaston Road, then turn left, and head south on FM 1464.
Map Location: WSB

109

A well-known poem by American poet Joyce Kilmer begins:

> *I think that I shall never see*
> *A poem as lovely as a tree*

Lovely pampered trees—and big ones at that—are the specialty at Bill Bownds Nursery. This is the place for instant gratification of the arboreal kind, if you want your home to look as though it has been nestled forever in a bower of live oaks or other trees.

Rows and rows of nursery stock in huge hundred-gallon tubs, as well as smaller tubs, present themselves for your approval. These trees really are the crème de la crème of the tree world: Each pot has its own irrigation system, thus ensuring that the tree gets all of the water it needs.

In addition, fertilizer is added gradually as well to make nutrients available constantly. Supporting each tree are rebar poles, so that even the summer storms won't uproot them. Pampered trees, indeed.

All of this means that if you buy a tree here, it should give you pleasure for years to come. After all, if you were going to invest in such an important part of your landscape, wouldn't you want the best tree available?

It goes without saying that the nursery personnel really know everything there is to know about trees. That is reassuring since you want this investment to have the very best start possible in your landscape.

Have you ever thought about planting a tree as a very special way to celebrate the birth of a new baby or to mark some other special life event? You could watch a live oak mature as the baby grows. What could be better for a child than to have his or her own special tree to climb and swing from?

Brookwood Community

Everything is top quality, plus you are helping very worthy and talented people support themselves.

Address: 1752 FM 1489, Brookshire TX 77423 and other locations

Phone: 281-375-2100

Website: www.brookwoodcommunity.org

Hours of operation: café, daily 11:00 A.M.–2:00 P.M.; gift shop,
daily 10:00 A.M.–4:00 P.M.

Directions: I-10 west to Brookshire exit, FM 1489. Go south on 1489. Brookwood is on the right.
Map Location: WSB

When you buy a gift item from Brookwood Community, not only are you getting a beautiful, well-made treasure but you can also be happy knowing that you are helping the adults with functional disabilities who produce these items. Started in the early 1980s on a large acreage west of Houston, Brookwood provides residential and day programs for these adults and is a model for other communities striving to have a similarly successful program. Most important, Brookwood accepts no government funding for its activities.

If you are thinking that this will be a small gift shop with bazaar-type items, think again. The gift shop and restaurant are housed in a beautiful, golden, Texas-style fieldstone building with wrought iron trim and a tower. You know that what awaits you inside will be special—and it is.

Not only does Brookwood have a large, well-stocked gift shop with all manner of enticing finds, but there is also a restaurant: the Café at Brookwood, whose chef is a graduate of the Culinary Institute of America. Citizens at Brookwood serve the appetizing luncheons, which include maple-grilled salmon, San Miguel salad, elegant sandwiches, and delicious soups. Reservations are recommended, and the café is open for lunch only.

After a leisurely lunch, it is time to wander through the gift shop. You will fall in love with the many serving pieces decorated with bluebonnets, the Texas flag, a black-and-white cow motif, or a patriotic flag theme. All of these items are shown to best advantage in eye-catching displays that tempt you at every turn. Out-of-state friends will appreciate the unique gift of a bluebonnet pitcher or tray—if you can bear to give it up. You can buy full sets of attractive dinnerware, too. Nativities, interpreted in many ways, are a specialty.

Let's not forget the books of all kinds, including cookbooks, garden books, delightful children's books, and religious books. Any of these would make a welcome gift or addition to your own library. For aromatherapy, try some candles that really do smell like the flowers they are supposed to represent or the scented Burt's Bees cosmetics. Several vibrant paintings of plants and flowers reflecting a garden

| | |

Retail Sources

theme are for sale. A sense of peace surrounds you as you stroll around.

Row after row of lovingly tended annuals, perennials, and tropical plants fill the greenhouses. Prices are very reasonable, and the quality could not be better. At Christmas and Easter, you can buy cheery poinsettias and regal Easter lilies, too.

Buchanan's Native Plants

Who knew that stocking your garden could be so much fun?

Address: 611 E. Eleventh Street, Houston TX 77008
Phone: 713-861-5702
Website: www.buchanansplants.com
Hours of operation: Daily 9:00 A.M.–6:00 P.M.
Directions: North on Heights Boulevard to Eleventh Street. Turn right on
    Eleventh, and they are at the corner of Eleventh and Oxford streets.
Map Location: NW1

On a warm, sunny day the air here is infused with the heady scent of roses. Buchanan's, which has been a mainstay in the Heights since 1986, is noted for its antique rose collection, as well as native plants and herbs. Antique roses do well in Houston, as they are usually more hardy and disease resistant than the temperamental hybrid tea roses. Here you can find a lovely pink "Souvenir de la Malmaison" and then get expert advice to help keep it happy when it goes home with you. Many varieties abound, both familiar and less known. And there are modern roses, too.

There is a reason that native plants are recommended by gardeners in the know: They are usually pest resistant, require less water, and have been proven to grow here. You do not need picky prima donnas in your garden, so why not give a home to a native plant? Altheas bloom for months with hibiscus-like blooms, and our native sages will attract butterflies and hummingbirds. Buchanan's also features one of the largest herb selections in town, including some less well-known ones.

Everything here is well tended, guarded by a couple of cats that patrol the nursery. Information tags on the tables are very helpful, giving both the Latin and common names, as well as culture requirements. Even though it is noted for roses, Buchanan's is a full-service nursery and provides all of the mainstays that you need in your garden.

The gift shop, housed in the cozy cottage as you enter the nursery, will lure you in. For those monsoon rains, why not treat yourself to a nature-oriented umbrella? For kids, there are "Buzzerks"—buggy-looking glasses. Or are you tolerant enough for an ant farm? A whole room full of bird-attracting items, wind chimes, and hummingbird feeders will help you deck the outside walls for our feathered friends. A good selection of books and other garden gifts is available, too.

TIP Before you head to the nursery to buy plants, do a little homework. First, does the planting area have full sun, full shade, or something in between? Then consult a garden book for our area for suggestions. Wherever you can, try to use native plants that have proven themselves here. Once at the nursery, make sure that the plants look bushy, green, and free of pests. Do not be afraid to tap the plant out of its pot to check the root system: It should not be wound around the plant. Finally, always deal with a reputable nursery.

Buds and Blossoms, Inc.

Color, color everywhere, from purple buds to pink

Address: 14120 Cypress N. Houston Road, Cypress TX 77429
Phone: 281-469-3378
Website: www.budsandblossoms.net
Hours of operation: Monday–Saturday 8:00 A.M.–5:00 P.M. (winter), Monday–Saturday 8:00 A.M.–6:00 P.M. (summer); Sunday 10:00 A.M.–4:00 P.M. (winter), 10:00 A.M.–6:00 P.M. (summer)

Directions: Highway 290 to Hufmeister exit; north to Cypress N. Houston,
the left
Map Location: NWS

Some nurseries look so appealing that they just invite you to come
in; Buds and Blossoms is one of those places. Everything in sight is
clean as a whistle and well maintained. That is really important when
you are dealing with huge numbers of plants since one little fungus
infection or bug infestation can wipe out much of the stock. As you
would expect, the plants are in excellent condition, leafy and lush.

The bedding plants are grown right here at Buds and Blossoms,
so they receive plenty of TLC right from the start. The folks here
grow more than fifty thousand flats each season, so their specialty is
producing colorful additions for your garden—and plenty of them.

To get your creative juices flowing, look around at the many
small landscaped "islands." These change seasonally, from winter to
summer. For instance, your winter garden beds need not be color-
less when there are low-maintenance ornamental cabbages and
kales in a rainbow of pink, green, and cream shades. Multicolored
pansies and fluffy white alyssum added to the beds will brighten up
even the gloomiest of chilly winter days. Summertime might mean
narrow-leaved zinnias, Gerber daisies in a rainbow of colors, daylilies, miniature cannas, and other heat-loving flowers.

It is always helpful to have information about the greenery you
are thinking of buying, and you will find it at the ends of the rows
of plants.

If you need a break from deciding which flats of flowers should
go where in your garden, rest for a bit at one of the tables and chairs
scattered around. Take a moment to look at the beauty around you
and gather some more ideas. You will be rejuvenated and ready to
go again.

The website is helpful, suggesting several spring-flowering plants
for both sunny and shady areas. Do not miss the "Fun Tidbits" area
of the website; it takes an amusing look at the virtue, or perhaps
vice, of maintaining a lush green lawn in suburbia.

Cabrera Farm Nursery

Come to the country for excellent bonsai and orchids.

Address: 3914 Cabrera Drive, Sugar Land TX 77478
Phone: 281-313-2000
Website: www.orchidsandbonsai.com
Hours of operation: Monday–Thursday 8:00 A.M.–10:00 A.M.; Friday 8:00
     A.M.–2:00 P.M.; Saturday 8:00 A.M.–5:00 P.M.; closed Sunday
Directions: Highway 59 south to SH 6, south to Oil Field Road, turn right, stay
     on Oil Field to Cabrera Drive; go behind house to nursery area.
Map Location: SWS

Sugar Land residents probably know all about Cabrera Farm Nursery; the rest of us need to become familiar with it, too. If you would prefer buying your plants at a real nursery rather than a huge Mc-Nursery, then get in the car and come down.

It's peaceful here; birds chirp overhead, and the wind occasionally rustles the leaves. The gentle lowing of cows grazing nearby serenades you as you wander under the tall pecans. You breathe a big sigh, knowing that the stress and noise of the big city have been left far behind.

The big attractions here are the collections of bonsai and orchids. Bonsai, which is an ancient Japanese art, means "tree in pot" in Japanese. Thus, it is the art of growing dwarfed, ornamentally shaped trees or shrubs in small shallow pots. The tree is formed so that it looks as though it were fully grown and mature. Growing bonsai successfully is not an easy process, and it is very labor intensive. The pot is carefully chosen to harmonize with the plant; rocks and other embellishments may be added.

The folks at Cabrera Farm have a whole cabin devoted to their wonderful collection of bonsai, and they are experts on the upkeep of these unique plants. They will furnish you with handy information sheets on each type of tree or shrub that explain everything you need to keep your bonsai thriving.

If you are looking for something floral, another cabin houses the other specialty here: orchids. These gorgeous flowers come in many colors, from the beautiful pinkish-purple color that we know as

Retail Sources

orchid, to rich caramels, creamy whites, yellows, and soft greens. Though they look like prima donnas of the plant world, they are surprisingly easy to grow in our warm humid climate. Again, you will get expert instruction on the care and feeding of these show-stoppers.

The bonsai and the orchids are not the only stars here. Cabrera Farm boasts a fine collection of native plants, including trees. Natives have been proven to be best for our area since they are already adapted to our climate and do not demand as much from the gardener. From hollies to hibiscus, there is a native plant that will shine in your garden.

Cactus King

An army of cactus awaits you.

Address: 7800 I-45 north, Houston TX 77037
Phone: 281-591-8833
Website: www.bluesguy.com/cactusking
Hours of operation: Monday–Saturday 10:00 A.M.–6:00 P.M., Sunday noon–
    5:00 P.M., but call to check since it might be closed on Sunday.
Directions: I-45 north to Little York exit, stay on feeder road, nursery is on
    right.
Map Location: N2

With its enormous red and yellow cactus looming over the lot on the North Freeway, this place is hard to miss, so give in to your curiosity and stop in. You will be glad you did.

Texans like everything big, and there are some big cactus plants to like at Cactus King. Gazing out at the thousands of large and small plants, you might think you were deep in the heart of Arizona, not Texas. Owner Lyn Rathburn says that Arizonans come to him to buy cactus since his selection and quality are so good.

Whatever your preference in cactus, you are bound to find it here. Thousands of plants cover the five-acre growing area; there are more than two hundred euphorbia cultivars alone. Other varieties include yuccas, barrel cactus, saguaros, agaves, tree aloes, monstrosed (mutated) plants, pachypodiums, astrophytums, and many more. While some plants are imported, many are grown to their full size on site in the greenhouses.

Cactus plants are perfect for Houston's hot dry summers since they are not water guzzlers. But if you are concerned that our occasional monsoon rains might drown a cactus, don't worry: They can take it as long as they have excellent drainage. As a rule, they thrive if planted in builder's sand, but check with Lyn when you buy them.

In a past incarnation, the owner was an illustrator. That creative bent manifests itself in the quirky, playful décor at Cactus King. Children and adults alike will be amused by the giant cockroach made of melted vinyl records. A land shark of concrete and bottles has wheels, not fins, for locomotion, while an amusing sculpture of stoves towers high into the sky. Some of the rusty-looking chests and sewing machine bases scattered here and there would be great outdoor containers for a single cactus or a group of them.

Did you know that some cactuses are edible? Tender young shoots of a type of opuntia cactus taste like fresh young green beans; they would make a tasty addition to a summer salad. Most people in the Houston area are familiar with the fruit of this plant, the wine-red prickly pear, which can be made into a delicious jelly or add a swirl of color to a margarita.

So come and meet the members of this fascinating family at Cactus King, see some playful sculptures, and take home a plant that is uncommon, yet undemanding.

Caldwell Nursery

A friendly garden home for unusual plants in Rosenberg

Address: 2436 Band Road, Rosenberg TX 77471
Phone: 281-342-4016
Website: www.caldwellhort.com
Hours of operation: Monday–Saturday 9:00 A.M.–5:30 P.M., closed Sunday
Directions: Just south of highway 59 on Texas 36
Map Location: SWS

The deep-throated sound of wind chimes that evoke Balinese gongs greets you at Caldwell Nursery. They are melodious background music to accompany you while you see the huge selection of native plants, rare specimens, and other greenery offered.

Caldwell's specializes in Texas natives, which have proven to be no fuss when planted in our gardens. Several of the shrubs and trees, such as the Mexican plum, and comically named farkleberry attract butterflies and birds.

The "collector's corner" showcases many unusual and rare additions to the garden, including the stunning blood lily, the flowers of which looks like exploding red fireworks. If you are a cook, why not grow your own allspice tree to flavor soups and stews?

A dazzling specimen tree commands your attention. It's a bauhinia, also known as an orchid tree, as you will realize when you see it in bloom: The tree is covered with purple orchid-looking flowers. This one is not for sale, but there are plenty of other trees that you can buy. If you do want a real orchid, they're here, too, and in great profusion.

Caldwell's stocks an enormous variety of flowering greenery, including some not seen very often in most nurseries. Two that come to mind are the amusingly named spotted emu bush and the deep blue–flowered Brazilian snapdragon. Availability does vary.

Sages of all colors and sizes do well in Texas, and you can choose from more than thirty varieties. Bamboo is gaining in popularity as a landscape plant; newer cultivars are more likely than older ones to behave themselves in the garden and not run amok.

Turn a corner, and you will discover new surprises. Pergolas, garden art of all kinds, birdbaths, and pots abound. Stepping-stones look like stained glass, but they are tough enough to step on. Adorable bunnies, pesky squirrels, and languid fish are also available as sculptures to scatter around the garden.

This is another of those individualized, smaller nurseries with its own unique character that dot our city. You won't get lost among the begonias, and you will find someone to cheerfully answer your questions.

Chateau Domingue

Choose a piece of the Mediterranean past
for your home or garden.

Address: 3615-B West Alabama, Houston TX 77027
Phone: 713-961-3444
Website: www.chateaudomingue.com
Hours of operation: Monday–Friday 9:00 A.M.–5:00 P.M.; Saturday 10:00 A.M.–
   5:00 P.M.; closed Sunday
Directions: Inside loop; Highway 59, exit Edloe, go north, then left on Al-
   abama. Go one mile, then left on Dorner Lane.
Map Location: W1

You have carefully planned your garden and now want to complement the plantings with some beautifully weathered French architectural accents, but a trip to France is not in your plans right now.
Not to worry, a short car trip will bring you to Chateau Domingue,
and you will think you are in the chateau country.

Several years ago, owner Ruth Gay was thwarted in her attempts
to find antique architectural accents for her new home. Rather than
settle for what was available, she decided to open a shop specializ-
ing in these age-mellowed antiques. Her hard work is your gain; gardeners will find a treasure trove of pieces to provide the perfect
finishing touch.

Chateau Domingue is a five-thousand-square foot showroom or
warehouse packed full of treasures. Some pieces were obviously
meant to be in a garden, such as the pyramidal planters that add
height. There is a wealth of fountains dating back to the seventh
through the nineteenth centuries, all softly weathered. When placed
in your garden, they will look like they have been there for centuries. Other unique garden accents abound, such as the baskets
filled with flowers and fruit that are captured forever in stone. Large
Italian urns, used for storing olive oil, can be a focal point for a low
stone wall or patio.

But the ideas do not stop there. Why not accentuate a corner of
the garden or a water feature with some old Delft tiles, with their sig-
nature deep blue and gray-white palette?

119

Retail Sources

Perhaps an antique carved door would serve as a dramatic entry into a garden room. Then, after a satisfying day of gardening, wash your hands in a seventeenth-century stone sink, knowing that you are preserving a little piece of history. You are limited only by your imagination.

Whether stone, forged iron, or weathered wood, these antiques will last forever. After all, they have already survived for centuries.

You are sure to find something to please your aesthetic sense at Chateau Domingue; the problem is setting limits on your purchases since everything beguiles your eyes.

Condon Gardens

Very special one-stop shopping in Spring Branch

Address: 7706 Hammerly Boulevard, Houston TX 77055
Phone: 713-782-3992
Website: www.condongardens.com
Hours of operation: Monday–Friday 8:00 A.M.–5:30 P.M., Saturday 9:00 A.M.–
    5:30 P.M., Sunday noon–5:30 P.M., closed holidays
Directions: On Hammerly, east of Wirt Road, before Hempstead Road
Map Location: W2A

You just know you will find the perfect treasure in the friendly, welcoming Dutch Colonial cottage that houses Condon Garden's gift shop. And you won't be disappointed. Moving to their present location in Spring Branch has given the owners more room to spread out and present their merchandise attractively. Beautifully weathered copper sculptural pieces by Bill McKenzie catch your eye immediately; they have a commanding and striking presence.

Browsing around the shop, you will discover the perfect cachepot for that perfect plant, birdbaths and other supplies to keep our feathered friends happy, garden art, and furniture. Books tell you how to keep everything growing, and there is even a selection of apparel so that you can look fashionable while you weed.

Let's not forget the plants: Condon is a nursery, after all. It specializes in organic gardening, and everything is in tip-top condition, proof that growing organically is not only better for the environment but also yields good-looking greenery as well. A giant staghorn fern would be a showstopper specimen plant in any garden.

Perhaps the sun does not shine on your garden as often as you would like; a good selection of shade-loving plants will brighten the dark areas. Planting mixes, mulches, and other supplies to keep your plants green and growing are available, too.

If you do not want to do the work yourself, Condon has an extensive landscaping service that will plan and then plant your dream garden. With fifty years of experience, they know what they are doing.

To quote their philosophy, they aim to provide "the perfect plant, bench, statue, gift shop item, and plant care need." That pretty well covers everything, doesn't it?

TIP Make a safe insecticidal soap to banish the bugs without harming you. Add two tablespoonfuls of dish detergent to a gallon of water. After mixing it thoroughly, pour some into a labeled spray bottle. Spray the plant thoroughly, coating both sides of the leaves. It is important to get to the undersides of the leaves since this is where bugs often hide and lay their eggs

---

Cornelius Nurseries, Inc.

Quality, longevity, and bushels of service—they have it all.

Address: 2233 S. Voss, Houston TX 77057 and other locations
Phone: 713-782-8640
Website: www.corneliusnurseries.com
Hours of operation: Daily 9:00 A.M.–6:00 P.M.
Directions: North of Westheimer, between Westheimer and San Felipe
Map Location: W2B

The "Neiman Marcus of nurseries" is how a devoted customer once described Cornelius Nurseries. Those of you who are familiar with both establishments know that the comparison is valid. Cornelius stocks the best of everything for your garden, and their customer service is legendary. Not only do they carry the tried-and-true foliage for the garden, but they also stock unusual cultivars of the more commonplace plants.

Having been in business for more than fifty years, the folks at Cornelius know their plants and can answer any questions you might have about their stock or gardening in general. For your convenience, there is even an information booth staffed by a master gardener or nursery worker. Dotted among the plants are cards that carry a wealth of information such as common names for the plant, its cultural requirements, and any other tips that will ensure the plant's success in your garden. Finally, there are information sheets about the most popular foliage plants, if you would rather have written instructions to take home.

As you enter the nursery, you will see a huge shady greenhouse housing a stunning cast of indoor plants that would make perfect gifts. Outside again, masses of annuals, perennials, shrubs, and trees tempt you to take them all home for your enjoyment. Do not miss the tables featuring bonsai and miniature evergreens; a mixture of these could be the focal point of a small indoor garden.

A useful addition to your backyard would be one of the stand-alone plastic greenhouses. Think of it as a handy camping tent into which you can move your tender plants if a blue norther cold front blusters through in January.

The Christmas store at Cornelius is very well known and offers a collection of vintage glass ornaments, beautifully crafted Santas, and quaint Christmas village buildings that will bring the season's magic to your home. Christmas-themed goodies fly out the door, while the experienced staff is busy creating one-of-a-kind centerpieces for all of your holiday needs. Of course, their skills are available year-round for any holiday or special occasion.

r

Community involvement is important here. Healthy plants start with healthy soil, so Cornelius offers a soil testing service to diagnose any deficiencies in your soil and suggest ways to cure them. They also sponsor a summertime tomato and vegetable contest, displaying the colorful winning veggies for your approval and applause.

Discount Trees and Shrubs

Instant lived-in treescapes

Address: 9755 Highway 6, Houston TX 77478
Phone: 832-328-0928
Website: None listed
Hours of operation: Daily 8:00 A.M.–6:00 P.M.
Directions: SH 6 south, south of Bissonnet on left
Map Location: W3B

If you want the instant gratification of large trees on your new property and do not want to cash in your stocks to do it, this is the place to go. The name sums it up: Discount Trees and Shrubs sells large trees—and some smaller ones, too—at good prices.

Keeping the prices low means they do not have a charming gift shop or theme gardens to inspire you. It's best if you do some homework and know what kind of tree you want or are working with a landscaper who can advise you about which type tree is best for your garden. Armed with that knowledge, come here and choose your tree—or several of them.

Stately rows of live oaks and other large trees in their hundred-gallon tubs are watered individually by an automated system, so you know they are receiving the nutrients they need to form good root systems and ultimately to flourish in your garden. Large trees are a sizeable investment, so it is essential that they be babied.

Good-sized magnolias are bedecked with fragrant lemon-cream flowers in the spring. Huge pear trees thrust their flowering branches skyward and will soon be sporting tiny pears. A large thirty-gallon redbud tree would be a striking specimen plant, especially if frothy white azaleas and pink snapdragons surround it as it blooms in the spring.

If the prickly leaves of cactus are a magnet for you, you will find some huge showstoppers here. They are so sculptural looking that, against all reason, you really want to touch them. Do so at your peril.

Let's not forget the smaller actors in this play, the shrubs, which are the workhorses of your garden. Loripetalum, with its deep purple leaves and bright pink spring flowers, can take our summer heat and is a nice counterpoint to all the green in the garden. Azaleas are plentiful and help soften the contours of a dappled-light area. Sago palms, which are not palms at all but cycads, are one of the mainstays of a tropical garden with their glossy fronds. They are lined up in long rows with not a yellowed leaf to be seen, so there are bound to be at least one or two you would like to take home.

The littler guys are here among their bigger brothers: fruit trees, including several varieties of persimmon, citrus, smaller crape myrtles, and more. Still, the first trees you see when you arrive are the taller ones, so if that is what you need, stop right there.

Donaho Garden Center, Inc.

Bringing the outdoors in

Address: 2920 Dairy Ashford, Houston TX 77082
Phone: 281-589-0037
Website: None listed
Hours of operation: Monday–Saturday 8:30 A.M.–5:30 P.M., Sunday 9:00 A.M.–
    5:00 P.M.
Directions: On west side of Dairy Ashford, a little south of Westheimer
Map Location: W3B

Donaho Garden Center's forte is definitely indoor foliage plants. You come to that conclusion after you pass though the main building and enter a series of interconnecting Quonset hut greenhouses. It's fun to wander from "room to room" and see what new surprises await you in each one.

Rather than trying to be all things to all people, Donaho's decided to do one thing and do it very well. Indoor potted plants, while not picky, have different light and moisture requirements than their brethren growing outdoors, which are rained upon or watered pretty regularly. The poor indoor plant has to depend upon a merciful gardener to care for it. In addition, if a plant does not receive sufficient light, it will wither and ultimately die.

There is a real art to growing greenery that is acclimated to the lower light and humidity conditions it faces indoors. All of the greenhouse rooms at Donaho's contain beautiful specimens that should do very well in your home or place of business.

As you walk from room to room, notice that some rooms are warm and steamy, perfect for tropical foliage. Others have large fans blowing and are air conditioned. The multiroom greenhouse concept means that each type of plant can be grown under the conditions that suit it best.

No matter what size plant your space requires, Donaho's can accommodate your needs. A small succulent arrangement in greens and grays could grace a desktop in the office, while a towering palm would be a striking statement in an atrium entry of a home. They stock everything in between, including showy bromeliads, cacti, and orchids.

Need a gift in a hurry? This is the place to go: Just select a pot and a plant, and you are on your way. All of the foliage is luxuriant and will make a beautiful gift for someone. Better yet, treat yourself to some lush greenery to soften your own living space. After all, you probably spend a lot of time indoors, so why not bring the garden in with you? You will be glad you did.

Enchanted Forest Garden Center and Landscaping

You'll want to buy everything in sight

Address: 10611 FM 2759, Richmond TX 77469
Phone: 281-937-9449
Website: www.visitourforest.com
Hours of operation: Monday–Saturday 8:30 A.M.–5:30 P.M., Sunday 10:00 A.M.–4:00 P.M.; closed holidays
Directions: US 59 South, exit Crabb River Road, south 1.5 miles. Turn left at FM 2759—do not cross railroad tracks—and go four miles.
Map Location: SWS

Breathe deeply as you enter the gardens of the Enchanted Forest. In early spring the fragrance of just-opened Rio Red grapefruit blossoms mixes with that of Carolina jasmine to waft a little aromatherapy your way. If you were not in a relaxed and happy mood before, you surely will be now.

A collection of well-planned display gardens makes for a pleasing meander. You can duplicate them at home plant for plant or use them as a springboard for your imagination. In any case, there is no guessing what that striking specimen plant filled with what looks like red baby bottle brushes is—the plants are labeled, so you will know it is a bottlebrush plant. The nursery prides itself on carrying unusual cultivars of familiar plants.

One of the highlights of the Enchanted Forest is a spacious garden room with decorative latticed walls softened with twining vines. You could get enough ideas here to landscape your entire garden, including the striking water feature they have set up. It is such an attractive and peaceful place that you might want to stay here for a while; give in to that urge.

A little stream burbles over the rocks as it makes its way through the property. If a stream is not in your plans, there are other displays of water features that would fit into even the smallest garden. Wrought iron pergolas and other pieces can give needed vertical structure to the garden.

Enchanted Forest has a truly charming way to showcase its plants grouped on each table: At one end of the table, upright lumber beams form the outline of a house painted a soft gray blue. Each "house" bears a label about the type of plant found on the table and is further decorated with a flowering hanging basket. This attention to presentation really sets Enchanted Forest apart.

Do not miss the delightful gift shop; everything is just as attractive as the foliage outside. The shop stocks all manner of baubles that would be great gifts—for a friend—or for you.

And did we mention that Enchanted Forest has hosted a wedding or two, in addition to being the setting for other happy occasions?

Enchanted Gardens

You will be entranced by all of the possibilities here.

Address: 6420 FM 359, Richmond TX 77469
Phone: 281-341-1206
Website: under development; will be www.myenchanted.com
Hours of operation: winter, Monday–Saturday 8:00 A.M.–5:00 P.M.; after day-
    light saving time begins, open until 6:00 P.M.; Sunday 10:00 A.M.–5:00 P.M.
    year-round
Directions: Go out Westheimer toward Fulshear until you reach FM 723.
    South on 723 until you reach FM 359. Nursery is at intersection.
Map Location: WSB

What could be more appealing than a rustic wooden bench attractively painted with the Texas flag and decorated with our state
flower, the bluebonnet? You just want to rush over, plop down, and
survey all of the eye-catching gardens and garden art around you.

Maybe you would like a bench in the shape of a farmyard animal
or alligator to enchant the children in your life. Find it and other
garden adornments here, along with chimineas to warm a winter's
night. Everywhere you look, there are homey items that will make
your garden a warm and welcoming place.

Enchanted Gardens does a good job of showcasing the plants for
sale in settings that help you see how they can be a part of your garden. At some nurseries, it can be boring to look at row after row of
plants. Here, the plants are grouped into minigardenscapes, with art
objects interspersed to show you the design possibilities for your
own garden. You walk up to what looks like a house with window
boxes, and, lo and behold, it's a façade. The real deal is behind it:
tables of plants, blooming their little hearts out. Walk around, and
enjoy the little surprises you come upon.

If tall trees turn your garden into a shady bower, a greenhouse is
filled with plants that do not like to sunbathe. The very knowledgeable nursery staff will advise you on shade plants or answer any
other questions you might have.

Since this is a full-service nursery, you can also expect to find

127

Retail Sources

fountains, birdbaths, pottery, and other additions that will give your garden your own personal stamp. No matter what the season, the staff can create one-of-a-kind designs for your enjoyment.

TIP In winter, the birds appreciate seed and suet, so decorate a tree for them. Mix peanut butter, birdseed, and suet to make a very thick mixture. Spread it on pinecones or small grapevine wreaths, and hang the decorations on a tree outside for your feathered friends. You can also string round oat cereal, raisins, or cranberries into garlands to hang on the tree. This is a great activity for kids during the holidays, and you will enjoy watching the action at your lively tree.

Garden Accents

Come to the source for a waterfall or fountain designed just for you.

Address: 15131 FM 2920, Tomball TX 77377
Phone: 281-351-4804
Website: www.gardenaccentsinc.com
Hours of operation: Monday–Saturday 8:00 A.M.–5:00 P.M., Sunday 9:00 A.M.–5:00 P.M.
Directions: One mile west of SH 249 on FM 2920, between SH 249 and Telge. Look for the white columns and fountains, then follow the road to the showroom in back.
Map Location: NWS

If you come to Garden Accents expecting to see water features nestled in lush, picture-perfect landscaping, you might be surprised—they do not sell landscaping plants. If, however, you want to choose the components of a truly custom waterfall or other water feature, you have come to the right place.

You see, Garden Accents is a factory; everything is manufactured on-site. Not only do they have a huge selection of components, but they also sell their merchandise to several well-known retailers around our city, as well as to folks across the country. A nearly unlimited selection of rock constructs, fountains, and fiberglass ponds in all shapes, sizes, and colors ensures that you can have exactly the water feature of your dreams, one that you won't see in every garden around town. The styles cover the gamut from classical to Victorian to very sleek and modern, with everything in between.

It is fascinating to rap your knuckles against a seemingly solid rock in a gigantic waterfall, only to realize it's a clever mimic of the real thing—and a lot lighter in weight, too. These waterfall constructs are very convincing, even up close.

A local artist who sculpted some of the fountains and statuary took his inspiration from the Mediterranean. Some of these fountains would be right at home in the south of France, while another spectacular example is inspired by a Tuscan fountain found in Florence. Several charming statues were modeled on the owners' seven children. Imagine the pleasure of knowing that your concrete kiddies are cavorting in gardens all over Houston.

You have decided that you can't go another minute without a water feature, but after that decision, things get hazy. Will it be the gentle sound of water trickling from a fountain or a lively cascade over a rocky waterfall? Don't worry; just put yourself in the competent hands of the knowledgeable folks at Garden Accents. You will soon enjoy the cooling splash of water from your own unique water feature in the garden.

Garden Dreams

Lots of inspiration and help with your landscape

Address: 13424-B Briar Forest, Houston TX 77077
Phone: 281-558-1112
Website: www.texasgardendreams.com
Hours of operation: Monday–Friday 9:00 A.M.–5:00 P.M.
Directions: Briar Forest, between Eldridge and Highway 6
Map Location: W3B

Retail Sources

Two tall palm trees sculpted in bronze guard the entry gate, marking the distinctive entrance to Garden Dreams, while hinting that garden design is of prime importance here. Although Garden Dreams' focus is landscaping, the display gardens, fountains, and garden décor items will give you plenty of motivation for creating your own dream garden. You cannot help but be inspired here since so many good ideas surround you.

An old-fashioned colored glass gazing ball would be a lovely bauble to add to your greenery. Hummingbird feeders in jewel-like colors not only attract these tiny bird, but also add their own sparkle to the surroundings. And you can have hummers hovering year-round in the form of metal garden stakes. If you are a true Texan, why not have a bronze longhorn to hang your potted plants from?

More good ideas: a colorful frog planter from Mexico, lily sculptures in yellow and purple, an iron bench in the form of a reclining mermaid, and cheerful Adirondack chairs painted with sunflowers. Garden Dreams also offers twig furniture with lattice seats and backs for a natural look in the garden, as well as twig arches and plant supports that are sculptures in themselves. Wind chimes add their melodious accent to the air as you stroll around.

There's a gift shop inside the house, where you will find CDs, cosmetics, and other nature-oriented products. And do not forget the plants: Metal gazebos and trellises cleverly separate garden rooms stocked with plants for sale.

One of the more whimsical landscape ideas is an area with a lush carpet of monkey grass with a glass ball that looked as though a child-giant had carelessly tossed it there.

TIP Have your soil tested; you won't learn its IQ, but you will find out what nutrients it is lacking. The cost is minimal, and you simply need to mail in a soil sample. Call your local county Extension office, who will send you the envelope for the sample. Follow the directions, then mail the sample to Texas A&M. You'll soon receive their recommendations for soil additions. Your plants will thank you by growing healthy and huge.

Garden Mystiques

Come and make your garden a happy place.

Address: 807 W. Gray, Houston TX 77019
Phone: 713-942-0010
Website: www.gardenmystiques.com
Hours of operation: Tuesday–Saturday 10:00 A.M.–6:00 P.M., Sunday 11:00
     A.M.–5:00 P.M.; closed Monday
Directions: Half a block east of Montrose on West Gray
Map Location: W1

You can't miss the entrance to Garden Mystiques on West Gray; it just begs you to come in and take a look. A tall fence is painted to look like a cheery, sunny garden, complete with azure sky, plants, and happy little critters flying and scampering around. Fluttering banners advertise some of the items inside; yard art and gift items entice you.

Once through the garden gate, you will see a world of possibilities for decorating your outdoor space. The most unusual would be the strikingly hued crystal rocks to set here and there, perhaps echoing or complementing your flower colors. Clear cobalt and glass-green rocks striated with white glow in the sun like huge sapphires and emeralds. For a softer look, consider pastel blue, lilac, spring green, or pale yellow versions.

Oversized concrete garden boot planters are not made for walking. Fill these boots with daisies for a whimsical addition to a country garden. Beloved by the Victorians, gazing balls in a glittering rainbow of colors add a sparkling touch to any garden. A benign sun plaque smiling down from a tree brings instant cheer to the scene, while a life-sized pair of ceramic flip-flops instantly brings back memories of the beach.

Several species of hummingbirds spend the fall months and sometimes even the winter in our area. Attract them with a jewel-toned glass feeder that is as beautiful as it is functional.

If you can tear yourself away from the outdoor offerings, there is more to see inside. For a quick gift, the possibilities are endless. Plant hooks need not be starkly utilitarian; these have painted flowers or birds. Sure to bring a smile, the flowerpot feet are available in

131

Retail Sources

many styles, including bare feet with painted crimson toenails. Imagine those peeking out from under a potted tropical lime tree.

Wander from room to room in this charming cottage to see more delights: chimes, birdhouses, plant-and-grow greeting cards, twirling danglers, wind vanes, sun catchers, colorful turtles and frogs, garden stakes—and the list goes on. Even if you are not a gardener, you know someone who would welcome a gift from Garden Mystiques, so come in and prepare to be enchanted.

Houston Garden Centers

Have a beautiful garden, with money left over for a chair to sit in and enjoy it.

Address: 5345 West Loop South, Houston TX 77081 and other locations
Phone: not listed
Website: www.houstongardencenters.com
Hours of operation: Sunday–Friday 9:00 A.M.–8:00 P.M., Saturday 8:00 A.M.–
     8:00 P.M.
Directions: North on West Loop feeder road, between Fournace and
     Westpark
Map Location: W1

Houston Garden Centers bills itself as "your garden superstore," and they mean it. Forget about choosing between a few begonia hanging baskets—they have dozens. And bedding plants? You could carpet the King Ranch with all of the colorful flats of pansies, petunias, salvias, and snapdragons they stock.

Stocking a large volume of nursery plants means that Houston Garden Centers can keep their prices down. At the beginning of the season, the prices here are competitive with those of other large nurseries. However, as the season goes on, you will notice that the prices begin to fall. By the end of a season, those same plants are often seventy percent off. Let the buyer beware, though; a deeply discounted plant that has been sitting in the summer heat for a while might not be the bargain it seems.

Keep in mind that the huge volume/low prices formula means

that you probably will not get the individualized specialty knowledge that you might at a small nursery. You might have to do a bit more homework about the types of plants you need. Also, there aren't always information tags attached to the plants or on the table.

The plants are well tended by an army of nursery workers, who water and maintain the stock. Nearly any type of plant the home gardener would want is available; these include—but are not limited to—palms, citrus, tropicals, shade plants, roses, shrubs, vegetables, herbs, vines, bedding plants, old favorites, and new ones.

Since they are full-service nurseries, Houston Garden Centers also stock the supporting cast for the flowers. Traditional clay pots and those that mimic clay pots, fertilizers, pesticides, and all the trinkets and tools so dear to the gardener's heart are here for your approval. When a blue norther blows in and the temperature plummets to below freezing, you can be sure to find plenty of freeze cloth for sale here.

At Christmas time, the centers sell Christmas trees almost as fast as they can unload them; the prices are good, and there is a variety of trees. Cheerful red, pink, white, and variegated poinsettias fill the store, so give in to temptation and buy several—they are priced right.

Go fill the back forty with daffodils, redbuds, tomatoes, or whatever you wish. You won't break your budget with plants from Houston Garden Centers.

Houston Palm Tree, Inc.

Forty years of bringing the tropical look to Houston

Address: 20420 Gulf Freeway, Webster TX 77598
Phone: 281-338-2658
Website: www.houstonpalmtree.com
Hours of operation: Monday–Saturday 8:00 A.M.–8:00 P.M., Sunday 8:00 A.M.–6:00 P.M., closed holidays. Between Thanksgiving and Christmas, open until 10:00 P.M.
Directions: I-45 south, exit Bay Area Boulevard. Stay on feeder road; nursery is on right.
Map Location: SS

For some of us, the rustling sound of palm trees is pure nirvana, not to mention the look of the tropics they add to the landscape. Waving languidly in the gulf breezes, they evoke pleasant memories of exotic vacations. Whether you seek a huge outdoor palm or a graceful indoor one, this is the place to find it.

You have probably seen the giant palms waving in the breeze as you drive down the Gulf Freeway toward Galveston. Although Houston Palm Tree is a full-service nursery, their specialty is palm trees, as the name indicates. Yes, you will find a huge selection of pampered nursery stock, masses of statuary, and ornate fountains trickling gently. But you have probably come for the palms, haven't you?

Here they are, some soaring into the sky like a series of exclamation points topped with foliage, some small enough for you to finger their lacy fronds. It is hard to believe you won't find exactly the perfect palm here, but if there is a variety of palm you want but do not see, Houston Palm Tree's network of sources can locate it for you.

If you are not sure what kind of palm you're looking for, just tell the helpful folks here what your ideas are. They will assist you in selecting the best palm for your needs and even plant it for you, if you wish. After all, planting a twenty-five-foot palm can be a little daunting for most of us. What do you do if you get it crooked?

Palms are at home indoors as well; they add a contemporary, tropical look to indoor décor. A palm or two in your family room are good specimen plants and are easy to maintain. For a stunning effect in your living or family room, use uplights to throw dramatic bold shadows on the walls.

Whether you want a lofty Alexander Palm or a pert little Ponytail Palm, create your own piece of the tropics by stopping here first. With their forty-plus years of experience, the folks at Houston Palm Trees can create your tropical fantasy right here in Houston.

Houston Plants and Garden World

Bigger can be better—and cheaper

Address: 16726 North Freeway, Houston TX 77090 and other locations
Phone: 281-443-3188
Website: www.hpgw.net
Hours of operation: Daily 8:00 A.M.–8:00 P.M. in summer; 8:00 A.M.–sunset in
    winter
Directions: I-45 north, exit Richey Road, stay on feeder past Richey stoplight,
    nursery is on right.
Map Location: N3

Everything is bigger in Texas, even our garden centers. There's a trade-off here; while you might not get the personalized service and encyclopedic knowledge that you would get at a small nursery, you will often save a lot of money. And if you are buying a flock of large oak trees or other large mass plantings, that's important.

Whether you want one specimen palm or several varieties to evoke a tropical theme, there are palms of all sizes here to suit your needs. Striking Bismarck palms, graceful Queen palms, curly stemmed Pindo palms, ribbon palms with waving fronds, and many other types and colors abound. To continue the tropical theme, why not add some glossy green sago palms? For a punch of bright color here and there, red or pink hibiscus are hard to beat.

But there is more to see than tropical palms. As in any good full-service nursery, you will find a wide assortment of annuals, perennials, fruit trees, and vegetables. Crape myrtles, covered with crinkly pastel flowers, are a mainstay of the Houston summer landscape; they fool us into thinking it is springtime when the mercury is topping one hundred degrees. Another way to visually cool your garden is to have a variety of shade-loving plants under your trees; there are many to choose from here, in their own large area. Since this is one-stop shopping for plant needs, you can buy garden benches, fountains, and garden décor items to complete the look.

You won't want to miss the seventy-percent-off, end-of-season sales, which start in October and November. The nursery stock is still very fresh, and plants in our area actually do better when planted in the fall. Over the winter they have time to develop a good root system, which they will need when the summer heat comes back in full force. So do yourself a favor and fill those empty holes in the garden.

> TIP Make some room in your garden for herbs. Fragrant handfuls of fresh oregano and basil will make your pizza sing. Add some lavender to lemonade for an aromatic cooler, or sprinkle a little chopped rosemary into gingerbread before baking. It takes only a moment to mix up and freeze a log of garlic and chive butter. Top a sizzling steak with a slice—it's a winning combination. Or just grab a handful of herbs and breathe their exotic scents. Experiment and have fun.

Jerry's Jungle Gardens

Jerry's a true jungle explorer—and we all benefit.

Address: 712 Hill Road, Houston TX 77037
Phone: 281-271-8612
Website: www.jerrysjungle.com
Hours of operation: Open only a few times a year for selected weekends in April, June, and October from 9:00 A.M.–5:00 P.M.; other times by appointment
Directions: I-45 north, exit Gulf Bank, west to Airline Drive, north to Hill Road, turn right onto Hill Road.
Map Location: N2

The lush tropical beauty of Hawaii inspires all who see it, but Jerry and Fern Seymour carried that one step further: They tried to create a tropical Hawaiian paradise on their five acres in north Houston. They have succeeded beautifully, fortunately for all of us.

Jerry Seymour told me he wants to stock unusual plants that nurseries are not apt to have. The Seymours' travels have taken them back to Hawaii and elsewhere in search of the unique and rare. Fern drew the line on a foraging trip to Costa Rica: too many snakes for her. Jerry, however, fearlessly goes where others fear to tread, bringing back tropicals that he propagates, thus saving valuable plants that might otherwise be lost.

A long driveway bordered with verdant tropicals hints at the wonders here. Bright green bananas wave gently, cannas are filled with blooms in red, yellow, orange, and combinations of these. Amaryllis, air potatoes, and other lush plantings add to the jungle appearance.

There are more than a thousand unusual specimens here, representing more than twenty years of collecting and propagating. Brazilian red cloak is a stunning plant that flies out the door whenever the Seymours offer it, as does blue ginger, which is not really a ginger at all but a relative of wandering jew.

If your garden is a shady one, it's not a problem. So many of the tropical plants have striking variegated foliage in many colors and shapes that you can add all of the texture and color you need. Just ask Jerry, Fern, or any of the other employees here for advice. In two seconds, they will be rattling off Latin names of plants like it's their second language. Don't worry; they translate.

It is obvious from their enthusiasm that the owners and employees have a real fondness for these plants and want to share that affection and knowledge with you. Although visitors can make an appointment to see the plants, you do not want to miss the sales held in April, June, July, and October. A party atmosphere prevails, good vibes and good advice flow, and the plants put on their best show.

Joseph's Nursery

Worth the drive: dazzling plants for a good price

Address: 3723 FM 1128, Pearland TX 77584

Retail Sources

Phone: 281-489-9786

Website: None listed

Hours of operation: Monday–Saturday 8:00 A.M.–6:00 P.M., Sunday 10:00 A.M.–5:00 P.M.

Directions: SH 288 south, take Pearland exit (FM 518) toward Pearland. Drive
    four miles to FM 1128, turn right, go two miles to nursery.
Map Location: SS

From all parts of town, it's worth the drive down 288 to Pearland to experience Joseph's Nursery. Plants here are all bursting with green vitality and look as though they have been lovingly babied—which they have, by an army of dedicated plant people.

Prices are very reasonable, and the quality is excellent. Joseph's grows their own stock in many cases, as evidenced by the thirty-plus greenhouses on site. This means your prize plant has not been languishing in the heat in a large truck en route to a nursery.

If you dream of strolling outside to pick your breakfast grapefruit or an orange for fresh-squeezed juice, dream no longer. There is a huge selection of citrus, both in flower and bearing fruit. Choose from many varieties of grapefruits, satsumas and other oranges, kumquats, tangerines, limes, and lemons. The Meyer lemon is especially appealing, bearing huge, round globes that are sweet and fragrant. Much of the citrus is produced in Texas, which means the trees are used to our crazy growing seasons. Who knows, the original fruit in the Garden of Eden could have been a fragrant citrus, like some of those for sale here.

Though we sing the praises of the citrus trees, let's not forget the other nursery stock. Row after row of carefully pruned roses stand ready to fill your garden with scent and color. Louisiana irises in spring and daylilies in summer will bloom year after year, ensuring constant color in your garden, and camellias will brighten winter days with their luxurious pink, red, and white blooms.

One greenhouse I peeked into had more geraniums in more colors than I have ever seen in my life. All were picture perfect, of course; I would not expect anything less here. Orchids and bromeliads attract those who love the tropical look. There are even bonsai, if you want venerable trees in miniature.

Outside again, row after row of thirty-gallon oak trees stand at attention, along with other shade and stone fruit trees, such as Sam Houston peach and Santa Rosa plum. Remember that choosing a variety bred for our climate will give you success—and bushels of peaches for cobblers and ice cream in July. What could be better?

Joshua's Native Plants and Garden Antiques

Prepare to be entranced by the beauty of Texas native plants.

Address: 502 W. Eighteenth Street, Houston TX 77008

Phone: 713-862-7444

Website: www.joshuasnativeplants.com

Hours of operation: Tuesday–Sunday 9:00 A.M.–5:30 P.M. (summer 6:00 P.M.); closed Monday

Directions: North on Heights Boulevard to Eighteenth Street; left on Eighteenth. Go five blocks west to Nicholson.

Map Location: NW1

Butterflies dancing among the flowers, birds hopping around looking for snacks, and hummingbirds swooping in jet-propelled arcs—this garden is *alive*. If that's the garden for you, then make tracks to Joshua's Native Plants.

Tables are massed with Texas native plants guaranteed to be irresistible to the creatures of the air—well, possibly to bunnies and other earthbound critters, too. Since Joshua is a butterfly and moth enthusiast, he can tell you exactly what greenery attracts each kind of fluttering insect. If you are lucky, the caterpillars will gorge themselves, build chrysalises in your yard, then emerge as glorious butterflies—all thanks to you. Kind of makes you feel good, doesn't it?

But there is another reason for coming here: the native plants that have proven time and again to do so much better in a garden than plants that were bred for another climate or raised in another area. You will be amazed at the variety and beauty of our natives.

The tables are chock full of a variety of salvias, or sages, all of which thrive here. Plants with lovely old-fashioned names like Moses-in-the-boat, ribbon fern, lion's ear, toad lily, sandpaper tree, and aluminum plant will evoke days gone by and perform well in your garden.

Poking among the foliage is like a treasure hunt. You might spy a sky vine, named for its sky-blue trumpet flowers, or a cluster of inky-purple elephant's ears. Cosmos in all shades of pink and red is underused in our gardens, yet it is an eye-catching, easy-to-grow plant and great for a cutting garden; scoop some up.

139

Retail Sources

Large informative tags accompany each set of plants; you will know exactly what is needed to keep the greenery happy in your own garden. Read these tags well; they present a lot of useful information. Australian zebra finches in a *faux bois* birdcage keep up a running commentary on things to anyone who's listening.

Keeping a watchful eye on the comings and goings in the garden is a dignified statue of Saint Francis, patron saint of animals and the environment; he must feel quite at home here in this habitat garden. Large bas-relief concrete stepping-stones add a subtle textural accent to the greenery. Tall jewel-toned glazed pots have been turned into bubbling fountains that can fit into even the tiniest patio garden. Next door at Inside Outside Antiques, you will find charming antique marble tables and other items to add the final touch to your indoor or outdoor space.

Don't miss the butterfly garden facing Nicholson Street. A showstopper, it is proof positive that an organic habitat friendly to birds, bees, and butterflies can be attractive, too.

Lowe's Water Gardens

Cooling splashes of water, with an oriental accent

Address: 17122 Stuebner Airline, Spring TX 77379
Phone: 281-374-9669
Website: None listed
Hours of operation: Tuesday–Sunday 10:00 A.M.–5:00 P.M., closed Monday
Directions: FM 1960 to Stuebner Airline, then north past Louetta near Oakwood Glen
Map Location: NWS

Nestled in a heavily wooded, naturalized setting in Houston's far northwest side is Lowe's Water Gardens. Water features, ponds, and fountains dot the woodsy surroundings, so it is easy to imagine how they would look in your own garden.

Oriental motifs abound, though other themes are well represented, too. Japanese stone lanterns are abundant, with azaleas and other plantings nearby complementing their beautiful simplicity. A candle or electric light placed inside one adds another dimension, reflecting and enhancing a water feature in your own garden. Graceful bridges can arch over a small stream or even a Japanese-style dry streambed. How about a fierce Foo dog to guard your home (an elegant way to strike terror into a burglar's heart)?

As you enter the nursery, you spy an eye-catching display of several fountains composed of enormous pots with water spilling onto river rocks below. Even an unusual large rock can be made into a water feature that will be a focal point in your garden. A large olive jar placed at an angle to send water gurgling to the rockscape below seems as though it would be right at home in the Tuscan hills.

Wander along flagstone paths for more ideas: four-by-five-foot areas are marked off with river rock of various sizes and hues, each with a fountain adding its cool splashing sound to the air. Some of these fountain vignettes are raised and bordered with brick or flagstone. One especially striking display has three large glazed pots, each spilling a smooth curtain of water into a pond. Simplicity itself for those who want a clean contemporary look.

If you have the room and the running water for a large pond, you can have two or more waterfalls tumbling over rocks that appear to have been there for ages.

Lowe's carries everything to bring the sound of water to your garden, so drop by to see their displays. They will do an estimate, install, plant, and advise you on what is needed to maintain your fountain or pond. It doesn't get easier than that.

Lucia's Garden

We dare you to leave empty handed.

Address: 2216 Portsmouth, Houston TX 77098
Phone: 713-523-6494
Website: www.luciasgarden.com
Hours of operation: Monday–Saturday 10:00 A.M.–6:00 P.M.; open until 7:00
    P.M. on Tuesday and Thursday

Retail Sources

Directions: South on Greenbriar, right onto Portsmouth, which is just south of
   Richmond
Map Location: W1

Lucia's Garden is a bit of the mystical and marvelous right in the middle of the city. You see this in the garden entry to the house, where intriguing little surprises wait under every leaf, around every shrub, and on top of every sawed-off tree trunk for you to find them. Lucia shows us that a garden need not be manicured; this one welcomes and warms you even before you set foot inside the shop.

Then you step into a peaceful, scented haven packed full of treats for both body and soul. All of your senses are engaged: Deep ruby or cobalt sun catchers glow in the south-facing windows, scented aromatherapy products soothe, while delicate harp music is a refuge from the city noise outside. All around you, filling the cupboards and shelves are charming bibelots that will delight your eyes and nourish your psyche.

Lucia's Garden celebrates the seasons: Small Christmas trees a-twinkle with starry white lights bring the spirit of the evergreen into all the rooms well after Christmas day. There is a full schedule of events and classes, some dating back to ancient times, that celebrate the seasons of nature and of humankind.

As you stroll from room to room, the soothing splash of water from the many small fountains accompanies you. In one room, a cozy sofa invites you to sit and thumb through a few of the inviting books strewn about on the cushions. They include a good selection of garden books, herbal books, cookbooks, and children's books.

Yes, this is a garden not only of the senses but also with actual plants for sale, primarily herbs. Along with the herb garden standards of basils, thymes, lavenders, and oreganos, you will also find many used for teas, such as raspberry bee balm and chamomile. Chocolate mint really does smell like chocolate peppermint candy. Large glass jars hold the dried forms of these culinary herbs, as well as many medicinal ones.

Lucia's Garden is a very welcoming holistic shop, one that caters to both the physical and the spiritual sides of its visitors. Stop in, and be prepared to pamper yourself.

The
Garden Lover's
Guide to
Houston

Nelson Water Gardens and Nursery

Cool down with all you need for a beautiful water garden.

Address: 1502 Katy, Fort Bend County Road, Katy TX 77493
Phone: 281-391-GROW
Website: www.nelsonwatergardens.com
Hours of operation: Monday–Saturday 9:00 A.M.–6:00 P.M. (winter 5:00 P.M.), Sunday 10:00 A.M.–5:00 P.M. year-round
Directions: I-10 west to exit 743 Grand Parkway, north to Colonial Parkway, turn west and go six blocks.
Map Location: WSA

When the temperature hovers around a hundred degrees, nothing cools you like the soothing trickle of a water feature in your garden. Whether you want a pond, waterfall, or fountain, everything you need is here. Rolf and Anita Nelson and their very knowledgeable staff will help you create your dream oasis. Their special "disappearing fountains" look very naturalistic; the water seems to bubble down into the gravel below.

You will find not only the nuts and bolts—and filters and pumps—but also the little extras that make the ordinary into something beautiful and extraordinary. Bog plants both soften the look of a water garden and keep the water balanced, which is especially important if you have koi or goldfish. And for sheer beauty, nothing can top water lilies, with their jewel-toned colors.

Reminding you that these are water gardens, touches of blue are everywhere. Blue pergolas define various plant areas. Cobalt blue and aqua glazed pots in many sizes are just the thing to complement yellow daylilies, red hibiscus, or whatever you put in them. A colorful pottery frog adds a bit of botanical whimsy to a pond, and a gazing ball glitters in a setting of greenery.

While you are decking out the water garden, don't forget the rest of the landscape. Since this is a full-service garden center, there is one-stop shopping for perennials and annuals of all kinds. Since they are grown by the staff themselves, many are unique and often not carried in larger nurseries.

143

Retail Sources

Nelson's is noted for its water lilies, thanks to the efforts of Mike Swize, who grows these lovely flowers. One of the lilies he propagated, the "Lindsey Woods," is named in memory of a young girl who was a family friend of the Nelsons. Some of the proceeds from the sale of this beautiful flower go to Texas Children's Hospital, a very worthwhile tribute.

Even the tiniest garden has room for a wall fountain. Add a water feature to your living space, then sit and listen for a moment to the gentle splashing. Ah, peace.

TIP Who hasn't gone out in the morning and seen the leaves of a favorite basil or lettuce plant decorated with holes? You can thank the slugs, which have been making their nocturnal rounds.

If you have pets, you might not want to sprinkle slug bait around, so try this solution to the problem. Cut the top third from a liter soda bottle. Put a spoonful of slug bait into the bottle. Put the top third of the bottle, spout facing inward, back into the bottle. If you have done it correctly, you will see that the slugs can get in but not out again. Staple around the edge of the bottle to hold the two parts together. Tuck it into a leafy area, and wait for your slug diner to attract customers. You can throw it away and make a new one easily.

Palmer Orchids

Lovely flowers, well cared for, and good advice for buyers

Address: 1308 E. Broadway, Pasadena TX 77501

Phone: 713-472-1364

Website: http://palmerorchids.com

Hours of operation: Monday–Saturday 9:00 A.M.–5:00 P.M., closed Sunday

Directions: North on Loop 610E to SH 225, east on 225 to Pasadena
Boulevard/Red Bluff exit. Stay on feeder through traffic light at Pasadena

Boulevard until Red Bluff. South on Red Bluff to Broadway; less than one block off Red Bluff

Map Location: SE2

As you step inside Palmer Orchids, you can almost convince yourself that you are in a tropical rainforest. Exquisite orchids surround you; some are like tiny jewels, while others are bold slashes of color.

Ray and Terri Palmer have been in the orchid business since 1977, growing and selling their specimens, which are heat-tolerant varieties and thus well suited to our climate. They prefer to sell orchids, not breed them, since many orchids are on the endangered species list, and seeds cannot be imported here.

There is an orchid here for you, whatever your taste. The Palmers sell both species and hybrid orchids, including *Asocendrum, Brassia, Cattleya, Dendrobium, Epidendrum, Phalaenopsis, Paphiopedilum, Vanda,* and *Intergenerics.* Quite a mouthful of Latin names, but all of them are stunning.

Orchids come in a myriad of colors, sizes, and shapes, so there is sure to be one—or several—to your liking. Maybe you remember your first orchid corsage in high school; it was probably a Cattleya and a luscious shade of pinkish-purple that we call orchid.

However, orchids are not limited to pink, softly shaped flowers. Some resemble cascades of dancing snow-white butterflies, while others are dusky, daggered flowers that breathe mystery.

Though they specialize in orchids, Palmer Orchids also has a good selection of calatheas. Strikingly colored plants that look as though someone has taken a paintbrush to their broad leaves, calatheas are colored, striped, and speckled in greens, silvers, and pinks.

An attractive lattice-wood pot with an orchid nestled inside would be a treat for a good friend or a cheering gift for someone who is ill. Palmer delivers plants inside the Loop, and there is free delivery to hospitals. They also ship to every state in the Lower 48. You will receive lots of tips on how to care for your orchids.

The orchids are very much at home here in the cool, moist air gently blown around by numerous fans. Babied and watered, all the orchids have to do is grow and look beautiful. Not a bad life.

Retail Sources

Paynes in the Grass Daylily Farm

Caution: This could be the start of a lifelong obsession.

Address: 2137 Melanie Lane, Pearland TX 77581
Phone: 281-485-3821
Website: www.daylily.net/gardens/paynesinthegrass/index.htm
Hours of operation: Open house annually in mid-May; call first or check
    website
Directions: SH 288 south, exit left on FM 518. North on O'Day Road, left on
    Olin, right onto Melanie
Map Location: SS

When you hear the word "daylily," do you think of the masses of orange flowers that were a mainstay of grandma's garden? Think again. With more than eight hundred registered cultivars and thousands of new seedlings planted each year, Leon and Paula Payne's daylilies come in so many combinations and permutations that you would have to have a huge garden indeed to have even a few of each kind.

These garden glories are quite different from each other not only in color but also in blossom shape. Some look like traditional lilies, with trumpet-shaped blooms, while others can have the rounded three-petaled appearance of an iris, with the other petals in the background framing them. Still others have long narrow petals that fold back from the center of the flower.

And the color combinations! Every mix of colors you could wish for is probably possible. Especially striking are the deep burgundies and luscious pinks mixed with pale spring green and cream. You can also purchase single-color lilies in creams, peaches, yellows, and reds—even a purply black.

Do you prefer a whiff of fragrance with your flowers? Want repeat blooms from your lilies? There is sure to be a daylily to suit your every requirement. In addition, you can plant lilies that will flower at different times of the season to ensure a steady floral show. Just ask the Paynes for advice.

The best plan is to attend the mid-May open house to see the daylilies at their peak. Then you will be able to see the plants in full flower so you know exactly what to expect when you order. You can also order online; e-mail the Paynes for a price list at payne @hal-pc.org.

Though they do need some care, daylilies are remarkably fuss-free plants, tolerating a variety of soil and moisture conditions. Best of all, they return every year to light up your garden space. What more could you ask for?

Plants 'n Petals

A blue hippo for good luck? Why not?

Address: 3810 Westheimer, Houston TX 77027
Phone: 713-840-9191
Website: www.plantsnpetals.net
Hours of operation: Monday–Saturday 8:00 A.M.–7:00 P.M.; Sunday 10:00 A.M.–6:00 P.M.
Directions: Westheimer, just west of Weslayan on north side
Map Location: W1

Plants 'n Petals looks like a little Italian villa right in the middle of the hustle and bustle that is Westheimer. Inside, you can find unlimited numbers of objects to decorate your Italian villa or whatever architectural style you may have.

The trend here is toward container gardening, some of it on a grand scale, which you might not find elsewhere. Huge urns abound, good for a grand gesture in a two-story entryway or two-acre garden. Many of these urns are already planted, a real time and labor saver, as well as a source of instant inspiration.

On a smaller scale, charming terra cotta roosters and hens can be scattered through your city garden if zoning laws forbid the real thing. There are also numerous large-scale water features and fountains, some with charming blue pottery frogs splashing around. Some have blue hippos, which may seem unusual, until you remember that the early Egyptians considered the blue hippo a sign of good luck—and we can all use some of that.

Hanging baskets are showstoppers. Best of all, they are all ready to accentuate your front porch or patio or to hang in a tree. And on

147

Retail Sources

that patio, why not have the pause that refreshes, with a charming Coca Cola–red table and chairs?

If you prefer to create your own design, do they ever have pots! All sizes of glazed pots in jewel tones are ready to be filled with your choice of plants. Baskets add a textural interest indoors or out, and rusty brown or more traditional black wrought iron pieces will add an architectural note to your garden.

Don't forget the birds: They would love to have a colorful mosaic birdbath for their morning splash. If you like the look of fantasy, consider a concrete bench supported at each end by griffons. Chinese Foo dogs will fiercely guard your terrain from all evils.

Gardens cannot exist without plants, but the embellishments you add can make all the difference between a ho-hum space and a warmly welcoming one.

> TIP Acid-loving plants such as azaleas appreciate a coffee break. Neighborhood coffee shops often give away bags of used coffee grounds free. Just sprinkle them onto the soil to a depth of half an inch, and spade under, or add them to your compost pile.

Plants for All Seasons

Personal service and attractive plants in the northwest

Address: 21328 Highway 249, Houston TX 77070 and other locations
Phone: 281-376-1646
Website: www.plantsforallseasons.com
Hours of operation: Sunday–Wednesday 8:30 A.M.–6:00 P.M., Thursday–Saturday 8:30 A.M.–7:00 P.M.
Directions: SH 249, exit Louetta, stay on northbound feeder road, just north of Louetta
Map Location: NWS

For those who live in Klein or the Champions area of the northwest suburbs, you have two branches of this nursery to choose from. The name says it clearly: They carry a variety of plants for each of our growing seasons.

The Louetta location is a pretty nursery in an attractive wooded setting. It is easy to maneuver around the small tables, and the flourishing plants are displayed to their best advantage. A rustic wood-latticed enclosure provides needed shade for those plants that prefer filtered or shaded light to blazing sun.

All of the plants are very well cared for, so you are sure to have success with them in your garden. Prices are competitive, too. And unlike a meganursery, where finding someone who can take time to answer your gardening questions can be a problem, the folks here can advise you about anything related to gardening.

Living in a hot area like Houston, we can't underestimate the saving grace of a good mulch on our garden beds. No matter how much you might water, the summer sun beating down will heat up the soil and evaporate the water quicker than you can say "rain shower." However, you might not like the look of a chunky dark bark mulch on a bed of delicate pink lacy cosmos plants. So before you buy a yard or two of mulch, take note: Plants for All Seasons has a unique display of dishes with various mulches and cow manures so that you can easily visualize the effect a certain mulch will have on your garden. Of course, you can always ask if you are still not sure.

Since this is a full-service nursery, you can expect to find more than green and growing things. Fertilizers, seeds, and medicines to doctor the ailing plant are available. Attract birds to your garden with a variety of feeders, and let the sounds of the birds blend with those of a musical wind chime. In the gift shop there's still more to explore.

TIP A shady garden can be as colorful as a sunny one if you choose plants with variegated foliage in yellow, white, silver, purple, or red. Look for caladiums, variegated hydrangea, white liriope, and red fountain grass to brighten up the garden. Tried and true flowering standbys, impatiens and begonias come in rainbow colors and will bloom and bloom with little care.

149

Retail Sources

RCW Nurseries, Inc.

Read, buy, plant, and enjoy.

Address: 15809 Tomball Parkway, Houston TX 77086
Phone: 281-440-5161
Website: www.rcwnurseries.com
Hours of operation: Monday–Thursday 8:00 A.M.–5:00 P.M., Friday and
    Saturday 8:00 A.M.–6:00 P.M., Sunday 10:00 A.M.–5:00 P.M.
Directions: Sam Houston Tollway north to SH 249
Map Location: NW3

Such a *friendly* place. Lovebirds and finches in cages trill without reserve, and a hen or two scamper around in search of tasty bugs to eat.

Good prices on familiar nursery stock and more exotic offerings make this a great place to stop for annuals, perennials, and trees. The trees, by the way, are grown at the RCW tree farm in Plantersville.

Speaking of trees, the dappled, tree-shaded light at RCW suggests that they have a good selection of shade-loving plants. And yes, they do have everything that is happiest when shaded from our blazing summer sun, including many tropical gingers.

For gardeners in Houston, RCW has one of the best and most helpful websites. At Christmas time, they feature quick and easy decorating ideas on their home page—good for the time challenged among us. Year-round, you can find out more about a tree, annual, rose, or other plant that you might be considering for the garden; just click on it, and you will see its growth habit, culture requirements, and usually a picture.

You might not know a soil auger from a soil test, but rest assured, both the website and the helpful personnel at RCW will set you straight. The soil auger and its companion tools are in good supply at the garden store, where you will find all of the usual supporting cast of fertilizers, fungicides, and feeds as well. There is also a nice selection of garden books specifically written for Houston and nearby gardeners.

If you need a helpful guide to what needs doing in the garden during a particular month, look no further than the RCW website. Not only do you learn about garden upkeep but you can also pick up some charming bird lore.

Having examined this very informative website, you will be enticed into visiting the nursery, where you can see for yourself the well-kept plants of all kinds that RCW Nurseries carries. Armed with useful information, you can then select those that will be happy in your own garden environment. They will flourish, and you will be happy. Isn't that what it's all about?

River Oaks Plant House

Playful topiary, sassy citrus, and stylish floral bouquets

Address: 3401 Westheimer, Houston TX 77027 and other locations
Phone: 713-622-5350
Website: None listed
Hours of operation: Monday–Saturday 8:00 A.M.–8:00 P.M., Sunday 9:00 A.M.–
    7:00 P.M.
Directions: Corner of Westheimer and Buffalo Speedway
Map Location: W1

It is hard to miss this nursery: The whimsical green topiary animals and birds along Buffalo Speedway guide you here. Giant peacocks, reindeer, and giraffes frolic on the grassy boulevard, a Harvey-like rabbit sits at attention, while angels add a celestial touch.

River Oaks Plant House is noted for its clever ways with topiary, an ancient art of creating living sculptures from greenery that dates back to the Egyptians and Romans. Topiary animals are a more recent variation. It is fun to watch a topiary animal come to life before your eyes. A metal frame is filled with moss, planted with a vining greenery such as fig ivy, then shaped, trimmed, and watered so that in a short time the whole shape is covered in green. Would you like a monkey to swing through your live oaks? Or how about a huge squirrel that sits obediently and won't eat the birdseed? These and other fanciful creations are yours for the asking.

The animal parade does not stop with topiary. A child would be delighted with a life-sized metal pony peeking out of a corner of the garden, just waiting for someone to go for a ride.

Fountains are everywhere, adding their cooling trickling to the scene. If you are cramped for space, consider one of the space-

151

🐦

Retail Sources

saving fountains that install flush against a wall or fence. There is no reason to do without the enjoyment that a water feature brings to a garden.

Maybe you have seen the orangerie at Versailles and want your own bit of France in Houston. You can do it with all of the varieties of citrus represented here. Oranges, grapefruit, lemons, limes, kumquats, and satsumas will give you intensely fragrant flowers in the spring and tasty citrus later. If you adore pink lemonade, there is a lemon that gives *pink juice* when squeezed.

Inside, you will find an extensive full-service florist. In a hurry and need a last-minute gift? Attractively arranged baskets are ready to take with you, or you can grab a beautiful bouquet already in a vase that will please anyone.

Robertsons' Nursery

Gather ye roses while ye may—from Robertsons'

Address: 2905 Pasadena Boulevard, Pasadena TX 77503
Phone: 713-473-1333
Website: None listed
Hours of operation: Monday–Saturday 9:00 A.M.–5:00 P.M., Sunday 10:00 A.M.– 4:00 P.M.
Directions: Loop 610 east to SH 225 to Red Bluff Road exit. Turn right on Red Bluff, right onto Preston, and left onto Pasadena Boulevard.
Map Location: SE2

As soon as you step into the gardens at Robertsons' Nursery, you know you are in a very special place. This is an old-fashioned nursery, not a "Plants R Us" type of operation. The owners, Pete and Ava Robertson, have chosen to concentrate on roses, are well known for the quality and variety of their plants, and are very knowledgeable about the queen of the garden.

According to their son, Pete, there are more than fifty-eight hundred roses growing here. That's a lot of roses to look through for that one special antique rose that you have your heart set on. Not to worry; a rose list makes it easy to find your heart's desire.

The nursery is divided into alphabetical sections, with each one carrying a certain type of rose, such as hybrid tea or floribunda. Within each section, the roses are grouped by color and are in alphabetical order. So refer to the list to find a rose, its location, and its price, then set out to choose your favorite.

This is a wonderful place to be around the end of March, when stunning colors and heady floral aromas fill the air. As you stroll around, the scent of roses especially noted for their strong fragrance wafts around you. Two that come to mind are the lively yellow "Gina Lollobrigida" with its heady scent and "Purple Passion," which has a citrus aroma.

Meander along the pleasant grassy paths, which lead to many attractive display areas. The Robertsons have a good selection of old-time garden favorites that have proved their staying power in Houston gardens. Deep blue flowers decorate the arching green sprays of plumbago, which is as close to a plant-it-enjoy-it addition to your garden as you can imagine. Bauhinia is a small specimen tree that should be used more in our gardens. But really, the rose is the raison d'être of Robertson's Nursery, and we are grateful.

In early spring, the folks here are busy pruning the roses before the spring growth spurt, thus ensuring optimum growth. It is obvious that these plants are lovingly and expertly tended. That means that any rose you take home has been given an extra boost so that it will perform beautifully in your garden. If you are unsure of the cultural needs of these beauties, just ask.

Southwest Fertilizer

Let them solve your plant, pest, and equipment problems.

Address: 5828 Bissonnet Houston TX 77081

Phone: 713-666-1744

Website: www.yardgeek.com

Hours of operation: Monday–Saturday 7:00 A.M.–6:00 P.M., Sunday 10:00 A.M.–
   3:00 P.M.

Directions: West on Bissonnet to corner of Renwick

Map Location: SW2

Retail Sources

The name is a bit misleading: Although they do have a good selection of fertilizers, there is also much more here. Their specialty is organic products; they would rather educate the public to try a gentle, environmentally friendly approach to a small problem rather than the elephant-gun technique of killing pests.

This is a place for vegetable growers who think big. Do you realize how many of those sweetly decorated little seed packets you would have to buy to plant a few acres of corn? Not a problem—there are bins of several kinds of corn seed, as well as many other popular vegetables. Just scoop out what you need. If you just need a packet of lettuce or marigold seed, that is here, too.

Ah, fertilizers—so many types, so little difference among them. Not *true*. The folks at Southwest Fertilizer will gladly steer you to the plant food that will do the job best for the particular greenery you are feeding. The same applies for pest control. The shotgun approach can result in all the good guys, as well as the villains, leaving your garden for more hospitable surroundings. So put yourself in the garden experts' capable hands, and trust their advice.

Macho types will drool over the stable of mowers waiting to buzz cut your back forty. Everything else you need to clip, rake, water, shovel , lop, chop, or otherwise minister to your garden is here.

Southwest Fertilizer caters to wildlife as well. You can attract the birds to your garden, feed them, house them, and keep them content with the supplies you find here. If you count yourself as a friend to the squirrel population, you can buy an adorable squirrel feeder that has a little table and chair so the bushy-tailed rodent can dine in style. If, however, you are not enamored of them, Southwest Fertilizer will be glad to sell you a squirrel-repellent potion. They really do aim to please everyone.

At the end of the day, when your hands are raw because you were not smart enough to wear garden gloves, treat yourself to some Udder Balm. If it is good enough for the cows, you know it will do the job for you.

𝓻

Statue Makers

The perfect finishing touch for your peaceful spot

Address: 2003 Blalock Road, Houston TX 77080
Phone: 713-467-9082
Website: www.statuemakers.com
Hours of operation: Tuesday–Saturday 10:00 A.M.–6:00 P.M.; Sunday 1:00 P.M.–
   5:00 P.M.; closed Monday
Directions: I-10 west, exit Blalock, go north; just south of Hammerly
Map Location: W2A

Maybe you think a classical Greek statue would add just the elegant touch that your well-manicured garden demands. Or perhaps Saint Francis surrounded by twittering birds is the image you are looking for. In either case, Statue Makers is where you want to go to see all of the decorative items that can give a warm, personal touch to your garden.

Don and Valerie Condon have been supplying these and many more statues, wall plaques, fountains, and other garden adornments for more than thirty-five years. The items are made of cast concrete since it is the best substance for outdoor use in a climate where we might have monsoon rains one minute and scorching sun the next.

All of the pieces are cast into concrete on the premises. Molds are carefully handmade and include architectural castings from around the world. The molds retain every scratch and detail from the original piece, whether it was made of weathered stone or wood. The concrete can take on a variety of finishes: a weathered stone look, a rusted country piece, or other unique washed finishes.

One-of-a-kind stepping-stones can add a lot to the look of a garden. For a classic touch, how about stones with an oak leaf and acorn motif? Or show your Lone Star pride with a stone in the shape of Texas, decorated with the state flower, the bluebonnet.

Squirrels, cats, and dogs are some of the other options decorating these stones. You can even have armadillos underfoot in the garden, if you would like—on stepping-stones, of course.

Wall plaques, architectural fragments, fountains, urns, benches, and other fine-looking garden adornments are plentiful. A unique

155

concrete piece can add just the right accent to the lush greenery in your garden.

> **TIP** Why pay for huge flats of annuals? Start your own seedlings in cardboard egg cartons. Begin by poking a hole for drainage in the bottom of each cup. Fill with soil, and drop a couple of seeds in each cup. Mist lightly to moisten the seeds, then keep in a sunny, room-temperature location. Check daily, and mist until the seedlings are the right size for planting. You might need to thin them if two come up in the same cup. When the seedlings are a good size, cut the carton into individual cups and plant each one in the garden. You will not disturb the fragile roots, and the egg cups will break down in the soil.

Teas Nursery Company, Inc.

The gold standard for nurseries in southwest Houston

Address: 4400 Bellaire Boulevard, Bellaire TX 77401
Phone: 713-664-4400
Website: www.teasnursery.com
Hours of operation: Monday–Friday 8:30 A.M.–6:30 P.M., Saturday 8:00 A.M.–6:00 P.M., Sunday 9:00 A.M.–6:00 P.M.
Directions: West on Bellaire Boulevard, inside Loop 610, pass over railroad tracks. Nursery will be on right, just before Newcastle Street.
Map Location: SW1

Did you know that the stately, arching live oaks, lush fuchsia azaleas, and other plantings that make Rice University and River Oaks so beautiful in springtime—in fact, all year-round—were two of Teas Nursery's first landscaping projects? New Houstonians would do well to take themselves over to Teas soon after they unpack the coffeemaker.

Teas Nursery has been at its present location in Bellaire since 1910, but the family has been in the horticulture business since

1843, and Teas is still family owned. That is a long time to amass gardening expertise, so John Teas and his family members probably know more about landscape elements than almost anyone else around Houston.

Yet Teas is a friendly, down-home kind of place, not intimidating at all. The nursery seems like a warm and welcoming garden where you can stroll around, get information, and then make your choices from the top-notch-quality plants displayed.

In late February, one of the glories of the Houston gardening scene is in bloom: the azalea. No matter what variety or color of azalea you prefer, Teas is sure to have it: they stock more than twenty cultivars of the "Encore" azaleas alone. Their user-friendly website tells you how to plant and care for these lovelies. Rows of azaleas are just waiting for spring to kick-start them into electric-hued bloom.

But we haven't even touched on the other plants found here. Cacti and succulents soak up the hot sun outside, while orchids, bromeliads, and tropicals bask in the humid air of an indoor room specifically created for their needs. If you are in a hurry and need to pick up a quick gift, try a many-toned calathea plant or any of the other showstoppers available.

Let's not forget the pampered and perfect annuals, perennials, trees, shrubs, vegetables—and the list goes on. Teas also has a large selection of those objets d'art you need to personalize your garden spot. And for a little light reading on a cold stormy night, how about curling up with a garden book and dreaming of spring?

The Arbor Gate

Get together with a few friends and come here—
it's well worth the trip.

Address: 15635 FM 2920, Tomball TX 77377

Phone: 281-351-8851

Website: www.arborgate.com

Hours of operation: Tuesday–Saturday 9:00 A.M.–6:00 P.M., Monday noon–
    6:00 P.M., Sunday 9:00 A.M.–5:00 P.M.

Directions: West on FM 2920, past SH 249, then 1 1/2 miles
Map Location: NWS

The Arbor Gate staff would like you to think of their nursery as a destination trip, not just a place to buy plants. It is easy to agree with them since you could effortlessly spend a whole afternoon here. Arbor Gate's motto is "More Than Just a Nursery," and although their plants look lovingly tended, the home and garden décor vies for your attention as well.

As you approach the first of the two gift shops, you are drawn to a large, striking, metal gazebo to the left. It is available for weddings, and classes are held here as well, although there is no picnicking. Imagine learning about herbs or roses in such a beautiful setting.

However, don't become too distracted because wonderful things await you in the gift shops, which, by the way, are invitingly laid out. Your eyes go from one roomscape to another, each one more enticing than the last. Bright, garden-themed paintings are available if you simply must have a pot of Matisse-like flowers blooming in your bedroom.

There are lovely old-fashioned dolls to perch on a chair in a little girl's room, and even the chair itself is for sale since they also carry furniture. On a whimsical note, there are framed portraits of dogs looking very regal in uniforms and sashes. Unusual lamps will enhance your interior decoration.

Once outside, you will find accessories to decorate your outdoor "rooms." Brightly colored Mexican pottery pieces line a table, and Venetian-looking gazing balls invite you to rest a moment in your garden. Large mosaic wall plaques depict garden themes and would brighten up a plain cedar fence. Any child would find irresistible the garden benches with a pig's or rabbit's head and tail.

Oh, and the plants. If you want roses, the Arbor Gate has plenty of them, all looking very healthy. A helpful feature is the demonstration gardens, which show you how the various plants grow and how they can be combined in the landscape. Everything is picture perfect, and the staff could not be more helpful and friendly.

The Backyard Gardener

The unusual in plants—and some carnivores as well

Address: 5117 N. Main, Houston TX 77009
Phone 713-880-8004
Website: www.backyardgardenerhouston.com
Hours of operation: Monday–Saturday 9:00 A.M.–6:00 P.M., Sunday 10:00 A.M.–
    6:00 P.M.
Directions: North on Heights Boulevard, east on Twentieth Street, nine blocks
    to Main Street. Turn right on Main; nursery is on right a few blocks down.
Map Location: NW1

Here is another of the Heights area's small, unique nurseries. You sense that the entrance to the nursery area is not so much an entrance as a welcome. A wooden pergola flanked by two latticed walls bids you to come in.

If you want uncommon varieties of tried-and-true plants, this is the place to get them. There are unusual colorations of many familiar plants, such as a Harlequin buddleia. And, if your taste runs to ferns, there are huge hanging baskets of staghorn ferns in tip-top condition, as well as eye-catching sedum baskets.

The Backyard Gardener is probably best known for its herb collection. The scented geraniums, which mimic lemons, oranges, roses, and mints, are well represented. Buy a couple containers of herbs; you will soon be hooked, and they will take over your garden. But that's all right; herbs are tasty additions to cooking and hold their own in the landscape.

Plants are beautifully displayed around the nursery, so it is not surprising to find that the Backyard Gardener folks are known for their landscaping skills. Since so many of the homes in the Heights area are older cottages, an English herbaceous border suits them just fine and is often what the homeowner prefers.

A little sign caught my eye: "Please Do Not Tease the Plants." Wondering what this was all about, I looked closer and realized I was in the realm of the carnivorous plants that Backyard Gardener is noted for. Venus flytraps, pitcher plants, and other fearsome plants

Retail Sources

sat there placidly, looking as benign as could be. But who knows what happens when they get riled up? Best not to provoke them.

The knowledgeable staff will help you put together a memorable garden and assist you in choosing embellishments from the gift shop, which includes some large colorful frogs. You will find the gift shop offerings irresistible. Go on; give in to temptation, whether it is a hand-painted tote bag or a softly weathered antique.

The Garden Gate

Find that one-of-a-kind treasure for your home or garden.

Address: 5122 Morningside, Houston TX 77005
Phone: 713-528-2654
Website: www.gardengateco.com
Hours of operation: Monday–Saturday 10:00 A.M.–6:00 P.M.; Sunday noon–
    5:00 P.M.
Directions: In Rice Village, on Morningside, south of Bissonnet
Map Location: SW1

There is no reason to venture outside the Loop in search of the perfect fountain, cachepot, citrus tree, or Italian tablecloth. You can find all of these and much more at the Garden Gate. They have a cornucopia of indoor and outdoor treasures to enhance your home or garden, including many that will give your green bower an English garden feel.

A sign on the front gate requesting that you "Please close the gate, cats on the loose" conveys the cozy atmosphere at this unique garden shop. Around every corner there is a new discovery to make: Walk ten feet, turn a corner, and you will come upon something to entrance you, something you decide you just cannot live without.

Statuary is all over the place: fierce gargoyles to ward off evil spirits or gentle cherubs to keep the butterflies in your garden company. As you walk through the various areas, the soothing splash of water follows you, demonstrating the many ways to achieve a restful sound in your own garden.

Ideas for decorating your outdoor space are everywhere: A gently weathered chair or rubber boot filled with plants makes a clever focal point. If you want a more formal container, consider the many antique urns and architectural accent pieces. For a touch of whimsy, it is always comforting to have a dog or cat around the place, even if it is made of concrete.

Approaching a small building, your eyes are caught by a sign that says "Please keep the door closed: Mosquitoes can kill the canaries, and don't let the cats in; the canaries thank you." I should think they *would* be grateful. Sure enough, musical trills fill the air, and small golden birds flash back and forth in their cages—a sight sure to enchant children.

Indoor décor is not neglected here, either. A garland wrapped around a mirror brings a bit of the outdoors inside. If you want to set a Tuscan table, you will find sunny-hued ceramics, vibrant tablecloths, and even Italian wall fountains to set the mood. This is a great place to break your budget—everything will tempt you. That's all right, give in; you'll be glad you did.

The Pineywoods Nursery and Landscaping

Plant a living habitat with their help.

Address: 12437 Sleepy Hollow Road, Shenandoah TX 77385
Phone: 281-681-2889
Website: www.thepineywoodsnursery.com
Hours of operation: Tuesday–Saturday 8:30 A.M.–4:30 P.M.; other times by appointment
Directions: I-45 north to Tamina Road. Take the exit east, cross railroad tracks, and turn right onto Old Hardy Road. Go to Sleepy Hollow Road, turn left, and travel three miles to nursery.
Map Location: NS

Even the name of this nursery evokes visions of cool, green woods dotted with shrubs and vines that house and provide sustenance for a variety of woodland creatures. The name is right on target since Pineywoods offers gardeners the means to create habitats to attract birds, butterflies, and other fauna.

Owner Jason McKenzie is carrying on an established tradition at Pineywoods. He told me that Lynn Lowrey, famed horticulturist and native plant specialist, had a nursery here at one time, where he trained many of today's well-known native plant experts. In fact, Jason is loath to clear away any vegetation until he can satisfy himself it is not a unique and an irreplaceable native.

Some gardeners think that if a plant is a native, growing easily in the wild, it has no place in a more manicured landscape. On the contrary, it will look and perform better than more finicky plants and with less fussing over. Best of all, many of these southern natives are decorated with fragrant flowers in the spring and festooned with colorful berries in the fall. Many of us recognize the American Beautyberry bush with its clusters of magenta berries filling its branches, but there is a white variety here, too. Rosy pink berries bedeck the Carolina Buckthorn, a compact tree that could be the star of your garden.

More familiar plants with fanciful names such as whirling butterflies, bat-faced cuphea, and Turk's cap share space with hummingbird bush, Mexican Plum trees, and strawberry bush. If you plant them, they—meaning the birds and butterflies—will surely come. A note on the strawberry bush adds an intriguing fact: The seeds, which really do look like bright red strawberries, are a favorite food of wild turkeys.

An Asian pear tree bends languidly over a selection of native plants on the ground below. Small tables are easy to navigate around and add to the homey feel of this nursery.

If you want a landscape that is a welcoming habitat for all kinds of wildlife, stop by the Pineywoods Nursery. They can plan your garden, supply you with the plants, and even do the hard work. Your lively, nature-friendly garden will provide you with many hours of enjoyment.

Thompson + Hanson

Well-known name in town—and for all the right reasons

Address: 3600 W. Alabama, Houston TX 77027
Phone: 713-622-6973
Website: None listed
Hours of operation: Daily 9:00 A.M.–5:00 P.M.
Directions: North on Buffalo Speedway from US 59, left on Alabama; nursery
    is on right a few blocks farther, at corner of Joanel.
Map Location: W1

Enter the nursery through an imposing wooden gateway softened by lush climbing vines. Pass by the attractive shade plantings, including pots of sky-blue hydrangeas. A left turn takes you into a stone cottage that would be at home in Provence—this is the gift shop. To the right is the nursery itself, as well as another stone cottage housing the landscape department. You would be correct in assuming that this is a nursery with a strong landscaping presence.

Thompson + Hanson has been a name to reckon with in our town for a while, and a visit to the nursery shows why. Almost any kind of perennial, annual, or specimen tree you would want in your garden is flourishing here.

Shade plants are sheltered from the sun's rays under a handsome wooden gazebo. Balled and burlapped Japanese maples are ready to become a focal point in your garden, perhaps surrounded with flowering spring bulbs or summer annuals. Perhaps a manzanillo olive, with its gray-green leaves and black fruit, would impart a Mediterranean air to the garden. An Australian import not seen in most nurseries is the pearl bluebush. Its striking, deeply cut foliage looks like it has been in a frost.

This is one of the strengths of Thompson + Hanson: It stocks plants that you will not find everywhere else. And do they possibly have nursery personnel that wash and dust the plants here? Everything looks spanking clean and perfect—a definite plus. Even the cacti and succulents look plumped, not parched.

A garden is composed of more than greenery; it must have accents of some kind to complement the plantings or containers to put

Retail Sources

them into. Thompson + Hanson has a variety of pots: large and small glazed pots in rich jewel tones, terra cotta pots in abundance, and soft-toned pots that look as though their nature-based colors are glowing from within. A pair of large old olive oil jars filled with rosemary would look magnificent flanking the entrance to your home.

The gift shop is filled to the rafters with temptations. Everything from chic casual table linens to charming Chez Panisse note cards and even the furnishings, if you take a fancy to them, can be yours.

Wabash Antiques and Feed Store

A step back in time that will charm you

Address: 5701 Washington Avenue, Houston TX 77007
Phone: 713-863-8322
Website: www.wabashfeed.com
Hours of operation: Monday–Friday 9:00 A.M.–6:00 P.M., Saturday 8:30 A.M.–
    6:00 P.M., Sunday 10:00 A.M.–5:00 P.M.
Directions: North on Shepherd, turn left on Washington.
Map Location: W1

Entering the door at Wabash Antiques and Feed Store feels like a step back in time to an earlier, more peaceful era. This is an old-fashioned store that sells all manner of gardening supplies, feeds and various products for your animals, and even the animals themselves: rabbits, chickens, and kittens. Several cats meander around, adding to the down-home atmosphere. You might peer through some lacy foliage and see a snow-white cat looking back at you.

Children squeal with glee as they watch the roosters strutting and crowing and listen to the quacking, honking, and cheeping of all of the other feathered friends here. You can purchase your own avian pets and bunnies, too. Food for these and other pets is available right here—crimped oats for a pony and food for Fido, Muffin, or the birds in your garden. If you even want to encourage the squirrels, there is food for them as well. Seeds can be bought in bulk or already packaged. To keep the songbirds happy, there is a good selection of feeders and birdhouses; even bat houses are available.

The
Garden Lover's
Guide to
Houston

Although the supplies for four-legged and flying friends are extensive, be sure not to miss the antiques part of the store name. They carry a lovely blue and gray style of pottery that will add country charm to your décor. A down-home wreath made of strips of rusty-red iron, a longhorn weather vane, and pails are just a few of the antiques that will give a sense of Texas history to your home and garden. Nothing is better than whiling away a summer's day in an Adirondack rocker.

Of course there are plants of all kinds for sale. Wabash Feed prides itself on its collection of organically grown herbs, including germander, feverfew, and others that are sometimes hard to find. In addition, an unusual striped lime, persimmon, apricot, and plum trees are waiting for you to take them home and enjoy the fruits of your labor.

You will also find a good selection of Texas native plants here. Information cards on the plants will answer most of your questions on how to care for them. Naturally, there are composts, fertilizers, tools, and other supplies for the avid gardener, including a good selection of organic soil amendments.

And a Few More Nurseries to Visit . . .

Arborgreen Nurseries

Address: 4401 FM 359, Richmond TX 77469

Phone: 281-342-7726

Website: None listed

Hours of operation: Monday–Sunday 9:00 A.M.–5:00 P.M., but closed Wednesday

Directions: US 59 south toward Richmond; exit FM 762, go north through Richmond to FM 359, turn left. Continue on FM 359 until you see nursery on left.

Map Location: WSB-Richmond area

As you drive along FM 359, you will notice giant yellow and green not-quite-real palm trees, marking the eye-catching entrance to Arborgreen Nurseries. This full-service establishment covers twenty acres in the Richmond area, near the Swinging Door Restaurant. The amiable staff will help you find what you are looking for.

Are you hoping to harvest your own pecans someday or maybe have a couple of trees to shade you as you laze away the summer days in a hammock? These and other varieties of trees might fit the bill. Landscaping shrubs such as sago palms can fill in the bare spots in your garden and add a tropical look. Flats of color plants will brighten up any area.

Ashley Gardens Nursery

Address: 21915 Kingsland Boulevard, Katy TX 77450
Phone: 281-392-1064
Website: None listed
Hours of operation: Monday–Saturday 8:00 A.M.–5:00 P.M., closed Sunday
Directions: I-10 to Highway 99 exit, south to Kingsland, turn left on Kingsland.
Map Location: WSB-Katy area

A delightful display of landscaping skill greets you at the entrance to the office at Ashley Gardens. Gather some ideas from it, then stroll around, and put together your own one-of-a-kind garden display.

Everything is grown on site, which probably explains why all of the plants are in such good condition; they are not shipped in from across the country but have the benefit of lots of TLC right here. Ashley Gardens is a full-service nursery, so you can get anything from twenty-foot-tall palm trees to flats of annuals to bring all the colors of the rainbow to your garden spots. The old roses are captivating, too.

Congo Nursery

Address: 2018 Strawberry Road, Pasadena TX 77502
Phone: 713-472-7408
Website: None listed
Hours of operation: Monday–Saturday 8:00 A.M.–6:00 P.M., Sunday 9:00 A.M.–5:00 P.M.
Directions: SH 225 east to Red Bluff, south on Red Bluff to Harris, right on Harris to Strawberry. South on Strawberry to Pasadena Boulevard. Nursery is on right.
Map Location: SE2

It is immediately apparent, upon entering Congo Nursery, that one of its specialties is hanging baskets, particularly those of bougainvillea. Row upon row of vibrant pink and deeper red plants bloom luxuriantly. Springtime brings a dazzling display of color, the owners' nephew tells me.

While the Congo Nursery is a full-service business, the non-foliage offerings are eye catching and even amusing. Stars, little and large, are one way to show your Lone Star pride; other décor items are variations on the Texana theme.

Ornate rococo fountains and concrete statuary are abundant. Perhaps your kids would like to share a bench for a moment with a concrete playmate. There is a very relaxed feel to the Congo Nursery, perhaps aided by the music playing and the palm trees swaying.

Covington Nursery and Garden Center

Address: 1905 Bingle, Houston TX 77055

Phone: 713-468-5596

Website: None listed

Hours of operation: Monday–Saturday 9:00 A.M.–6:00 P.M., Sunday 10:00 A.M.–
 5:00 P.M.

Directions: On Bingle, north of Long Point

Map Location: W2A

A familiar neighborhood name, Covington Nursery has been a part of Spring Branch since the 1950s. At that time, Spring Branch was a suburb of Houston with plenty of green space around it. Today the city has grown up around Covington, which remains well situated in a convenient location for residents of Spring Branch and the Memorial Villages.

The nursery stock is shipshape, evidence of the TLC they give their plants. There is a room of succulents and tropicals, any one of which would make a welcome gift for a friend. Combine it with an attractive holder or other bauble from the gift shop, and you have a winner.

Discount Trees of Brenham

Address: 2800 N. Park Street, Brenham TX 77833

Phone: 979-836-7225

Website: not listed

Hours of operation: Tuesday–Saturday 9:00 A.M.–5:00 P.M.; closed Sunday and
Monday

Directions: US 290 to Brenham, turn right onto FM 577. At SH 36 (N. Park
Street), turn right, and go one mile north to the nursery, which is on the
east side of N. Park Street.

Map Location: NWS-Brenham

Like soldiers on parade, the rows of trees stand ramrod straight at Discount Trees of Brenham. And like soldiers, whose dress uniforms are bandbox neat, these trees are in the best of condition—watered, fed, and lovingly tended so that you can take home the healthiest tree imaginable.

The selection includes more than thirty varieties of shade trees, half of which are Texas natives. You can then fill in with understory trees—ornamentals, fruit and nut trees, and other smaller trees. Finally, come down to earth with shrubs, grasses, groundcovers, and perennials.

It is worth noting that the nursery stock at Discount Trees is weighted heavily toward Texas natives. You will be one step ahead of the game when you plant natives since they have already shown they like the conditions in our state just fine.

Frank's Nursery

Address: 302 FM 359, Richmond TX 77469

Phone: 281-342-3211

Website: None listed

Hours of operation: Monday–Saturday 7:30 A.M.–6:00 P.M., Sunday 10:00 A.M.–
5:00 P.M.

Directions: Alternate US 90 to FM 359. North on 359 to nursery.

Map Location: WSB-Richmond area

A neighborhood spot in Richmond, Frank's Nursery is noted for its great selection of tropical plants. Stop in, and you can walk out with enough varied foliage to create your own tropical rainforest. Or, if you wish, they can design a landscape plan for you and do the work. All you need do is provide yourself with a cushy chaise lounge and fruity drink to enjoy the scene when it is completed.

The employees are very helpful, answering your every question. The nursery stock is well taken care of, so you will be getting nice, healthy plants.

JRN's Nursery II

Address: 11701 Alief Clodine, Houston TX 77072

Phone: 281-235-3460

Website: None listed

Hours of operation: Monday–Saturday 8:30 A.M.–8:00 P.M., Sunday 9:00 A.M.–6:30 P.M.

Directions: Sam Houston Tollway south to Westpark exit. Stay on feeder road until Harwin. Turn right on Harwin, which becomes Alief Clodine Road.

Map Location: W3B

Do you know the Vietnamese word for "green tea plant"? It's *trà lá xanh*. JRN's caters to the Asian population in west Houston with a wide selection of greenery familiar to them from their native countries. Among them are the *Michelia alba*, a graceful and very fragrant specimen shrub and the tasty June plum. Of special interest is the Mickey Mouse plant, which, when lavishly decorated, plays a leading role in the Vietnamese and Chinese new year celebrations. The yellow flowers give way to black berries suspended from red sepals, which seem to resemble Mickey.

Citrus trees are abundant; grapefruit decked the branches of trees like small green soccer balls; they will be ready in winter. Limes, kumquats, tangerines, mandarins, tangelos, lemons, ugli fruit—they are all here and make great additions to both your garden and daily diet.

Stop by JRN's for the exotic, for the familiar, and for the friendliness.

Legacy Live Oak Farms, Inc.

Address: 3546 Harkey Road, Pearland TX 77584

Phone: 281-489-7179

Website: www.legacyoakfarm.com

Hours of operation: Monday-Friday 8:00 A.M.–5:00 P.M. (closed for lunch, noon–1:00 P.M.); closed Saturday and Sunday

Directions: South on TX 288, exit at FM 518, head east to Harkey Road, south on Harkey

Map Location: SS

If you plan to stroll around looking at the healthy trees here, plan for a long stroll, for there are seventeen acres of several varieties of oaks, plus any other landscape tree you might desire. Among the more than fifty kinds of trees, you are sure to find a few to grace your garden.

Rows of trees stand at attention in their huge containers that have built-in water and nutrient supplies. These trees are bursting with health and will give you much enjoyment for years to come. Stop by, and maybe one of the golf carts can ferry you around to make your decision-making easier on your feet. Much of their business is wholesale, but retail customers are graciously welcomed, too.

Nature's Touch Garden Center

Address: 5165 Louetta Road, Spring TX 77379

Phone: 281-655-7171

Website: None listed

Hours of operation: Spring and summer, daily 9:00 A.M.–6:00 P.M.; winter, daily 9:00 A.M.–5:30 P.M.

Directions: I-45 north to Cypresswood exit, west on Cypresswood to Kuykendahl, north to Louetta, left on Louetta

Map Location: NWS

Cozily nestled in the trees of Houston's northwest side since 1999 is Nature's Touch, a pleasant place to spend some time. The main building is a light-filled space that houses the gift shop and garden essentials like fertilizers and seeds.

Outside, wrought iron constructions such as archways, table and chair sets, and planter's and baker's racks suggest ways to incorporate these sculptural accents into your own garden. A nod to holistic gardening is the attractive display of plants that will entice butterflies to call your garden home, and there's a good selection of herbs, too.

San Jacinto Stone

Address: 195 Yale Street, Houston TX 77007
Phone: 713-868-3466
Website: www.sanjacintostone.com
Hours of operation: Monday–Friday 8:00 A.M.–5:00 P.M., Saturday 9:00 A.M.–
    3:00 P.M., closed Sunday
Directions: One block south of I-10 on Yale in the Heights
Map Location: W1

Rocks—did you ever think they could be so fascinating and varied? San Jacinto Stone is the largest stone company in the state, and they have a huge selection of stone for whatever you need. It does not matter whether you are just flagging a small patio, either; you will still get great selection and service.

Flagstones, accent rocks, borders for your gardens, and crushed gravel—everything is here. All right, stones can't be lovingly tended like flowers, but they are still an important part of the garden landscape, so you owe it to yourself to stop in for some hardscaping to embellish your garden.

Spring Creek Daylily Garden

Address: 25150 Gosling, Spring TX 77389
Phone: 281-351-8827
Website: None listed
Hours of operation: call for appointment or catalog
Directions: I-45 north to exit 70A, continue north on feeder road to FM 2920,
    turn west toward Tomball, and go about five miles to Gosling. North on
    Gosling 4_ miles to the garden
Map Location: NWS

Are you wild about daylilies? Then you have to see them in all their glory at Spring Creek Daylily Garden, preferably in the late spring when they are blooming. Since Mary Gage raises and sells more than three hundred cultivars, many of which she developed herself, you are sure to find your heart's desire blooming here.

The names themselves are enticing—Lady Marmalade and Fire-breathing Dragon—but the flowers are even more alluring. Every shape, whether spiderlike or with full rounded petals, is available. The color combinations are dizzying: Each unusually striking daylily vies for your attention. Why resist? Order several, and before you know it, they will arrive in perfect condition, ready to plant and enjoy for years to come, with only minimal care and feeding involved. You can't ask for more than that, so get out to Spring Creek Daylily Garden, and get ready to fall in love with daylilies.

Sun-Land Nursery

Address: 402 FM 646, League City TX 77574

Phone: 281-337-1024

Website: None listed

Hours of operation: Monday–Saturday 8:00 A.M.–5:30 P.M., Sunday 9:00 A.M.–5:00 P.M.

Directions: I-45 south, exit Highway 646, go east. Nursery is on south side between I-45 and SH 3.

Map Location: SES

Sun-Land has everything from soup to nuts, horticulturally speaking. Right at the entrance to the nursery are labeled, cubic-yard samples of many kinds of rocks and stone, from large "designer rocks" to small gray-green river rock and everything in between. Once you have decided on the underpinnings of the garden, it is time to choose the foliage that will soften the look.

Quonset hut structures house some of the shade-loving specimens, while the sun worshippers catch the breeze outside. The soft clattering sound of palm fronds is an invitation to buy one of these stately trees. Oaks, citrus, crape myrtles, smaller shrubs, and annual bedding plants round out the offerings here. Sun-Land is a good place to find both rocks and phlox.

Tall Plants

Address: 9191 Katy Freeway, Houston TX 77024

Phone: 713-464-8671

Website: None listed

Hours of operation: Monday–Friday 10:00 A.M.–5:30 P.M., Saturday
    10:00 A.M.–5:00 P.M., Sunday noon–5:00 P.M.

Directions: I-10 west to Bingle exit, U-turn on feeder road. Tall Plants is be-
    fore you get to Campbell Road.

Map Location: W2B

Since 1977, Tall Plants has been the source for . . . very large plants.
As the name suggests, there are numerous tall specimen and accent
plants for your soaring entryway, bedroom, or business location.

Because so many of these plants will enjoy life in air-conditioned
settings, there is a great selection of shade lovers. Prices are reasonable, and the plants seem happy. Large "baskets" made of logs would
be a striking focal point when filled with equally large plants.

Books for Houston Gardeners

Unless you were the landscape artist of the Garden of Eden, at some point you will need some good garden books to refer to for advice. Aside from that, they are all just so beautiful to page through.

An important point to remember is that many garden books are written for a temperate climate with four definite and pronounced seasons. While these books are certainly useful for general gardening knowledge, take some of the advice with a very large grain or two of salt. In other words, if you wait until April or May to plant tomatoes, you have missed the boat; ours go into the ground in early March—or even February if you are feeling particularly lucky. By June they're finished, but we can plant them again in August for a late-October harvest.

With that in mind, here are my recommendations for gardening books that can form the core of your Houston gardening library. They cover every topic you would want to read about and avoid most of the pitfalls that await you if you rely solely on that well-thumbed gardening book from Seattle. You can be sure the authors are knowledgeable about gardening in our area. Each book is a good read, an entertaining and informative companion to curl up with on a chilly winter afternoon.

Other books can be added as your interest and curiosity demand, but these will get you started. And always remember that a quick answer to a gardening question is as near as the phone line of the county extension service where you live, your local nursery, or a good friend.

Good Garden Books for Your Library

All about Trees: In and Around Houston, by John Foster. 1998. Swan Publishing.

Antique Roses for the South, new edition, by William Welch. 1990. Taylor Trade Publishing.

Attracting Birds to Southern Gardens, by Thomas Pope, Neil Odenwald, and Charles Fryling Jr. 1993. Taylor Publishing.

Bulbs for Warm Climates, by Thad Howard. 2001. University of Texas Press.

Butterflies of Houston and Southeast Texas, by John Tveten and Gloria Tveten. 1996. University of Texas Press.

Butterfly Gardening for the South, by Geyata Ajilvsgi. 1991. Taylor Trade Publishing.

Commonsense Vegetable Gardening for the South, by William D. Adams and Thomas Leroy. 1995. Taylor Publishing.

Dear Dirt Doctor: Questions Answered the Natural Way, by J. Howard Garrett and C. Malcolm Beck. 2003. University of Texas Press.

Garden Book for Houston and the Gulf Coast, A, by River Oaks Garden Club. 2002. Gulf Publishing.

Gardener's Guide to Growing Bulbs on the Gulf Coast, A, by Sally McQueen Squire. 1998. River Bend Publishing.

Gardening with Native Plants of the South, by Sally Wasowski, with Andy Wasowski. 1994. Taylor Trade Publishing.

Gardening with Nature in Texas, by Karen Breneman. 2002. Republic of Texas.

Growing Fruits and Nuts in the South: The Definitive Guide, by

The
Garden Lover's
Guide to
Houston

William D. Adams and Thomas LeRoy. 1992. Taylor Publishing.

Habitat Gardening for Houston and Southeast Texas, by Mark Bowen and Mary Bowen. 1988. River Bend Publishing.

Herb Gardening in Texas, by Sol Meltzer. 1997. Gulf Publishing.

Herbs for Texas, by J. Howard Garrett. 2001. University of Texas Press.

Houston Garden Book, by John Kriegel and the editors of *Houston Home and Garden* magazine. 1991. Shearer Publishing.

How to Grow Native Plants of Texas and the Southwest, by Jill Nokes. 2001. University of Texas Press.

Howard Garrett's Plants for Texas, by J. Howard Garrett. 1996. University of Texas Press.

Landscaping with Native Plants of Texas, by George Miller. 2006. Voyageur Press.

Lazy Gardener's Guide, The, by Brenda Beust Smith. 1997. River Bend Publishing.

Lone Star Gardener's Book of Lists, The, by William D. Adams. 2000. Taylor Trade Publishing.

Native Texas Plants: Landscaping Region by Region, by Sally Wasowski, with Andy Wasowski. 2002. Gulf Publishing.

Neil Sperry's Complete Guide to Texas Gardens, by Neil Sperry. 1991. Taylor Trade Publishing.

Organic Rose Garden, The, by Liz Druitt. 2004. Taylor Publishing.

Perennial Garden Color, by William Welch. 1989. Taylor Publishing.

Perennial Gardens for Texas, by Julie Ryan. 1998. University of Texas Press.

Roses in the Southern Garden, by G. Michael Shoup. 2000. Antique Rose Emporium.

Southern Heirloom Garden, The, by William Welch and Greg Grant. 1995. Taylor Trade Publishing.

Southern Herb Growing, by Madalene Hill and Gwen Barclay, with Jean Hardy. 1997. Shearer Publishing.

Sunset Western Garden Book, by Kathleen Norris Brenzel (editor). 2001. Sunset Books.

Texas Bug Book: The Good, the Bad, and the Ugly, by C. Malcolm Beck and J. Howard Garrett. 2005. University of Texas Press.

Texas Flower Garden, The, by Kathy Huber. 2005. Gibbs Smith Publishers.

Texas Flowerscaper, The, by Kathy Huber. 1996. Gibbs Smith Publishers.

Texas Gardening the Natural Way, by J. Howard Garrett. 2004. University of Texas Press.

Texas Organic Vegetable Gardening, by J. Howard Garrett and C. Malcolm Beck. 1998. Gulf Publishing.

Texas Trees, by J. Howard Garrett. 2002. Taylor Trade Publishing.

Vegetable Book: A Texan's Guide to Gardening, The, by Sam Cotner. 1986. Texas Monthly Press.

Year Round Vegetables, Fruits, and Flowers from Metro Houston: A Natural Organic Approach Using Ecology, by Bob Randall. 2001. Year Round Gardening Press.

Helpful Websites

I f you Google the word "gardening," your search yields millions of entries, some of which are useful, some not. Here are some of the better ones, which often have links to other good sites.

One of the best for this area is the Texas A&M website, where you can even click on a rogues' gallery of the critters that are eating your tomatoes before you even have a chance to savor the fruit. Everything and more about gardening is on this site. Two especially good links are the Texas Superstars, plants that perform especially well in our climate, and the PlantAnswers link, which answers questions you did not even know you had. Information about the Master Gardener program is here as well.

Did you see a glorious blue-flowered tropical plant in Hawaii that you want to identify so you can add it to your tropical paradise at home? Try one of the search sites listed, or Google the common name and select images to see whether it is the plant you are looking for.

Many websites have a wealth of good general gardening information; some include gardeners' forums where you can rejoice with other kindred souls about your successes or commiserate with them about an occasional failure. Seed and plant exchanges are featured on some sites. They are a wonderful way of obtaining a rare plant or a "pass along" addition for your garden.

Most useful of all are the sites dedicated to gardening in the Houston area. You can be sure the information is targeted to the conditions here. In addition, local gardening events worth attending are usually highlighted on these sites. The chapter about garden clubs and societies already has the relevant websites listed there. And to help make a weekend getaway even more enjoyable, valuable sites for some tourist destinations in the Day Trips chapter are included here.

Let's not forget that there is always room for fun. A few offbeat or zany sites and some helpful ones are here for your amusement or education—enjoy them.

Finally, stop and visit my website, www.houstongardenlover.com. Pick up some garden tips, as well as food, travel, and wine lore. Visit often and share your ideas.

A Few Sites to Get You Started

The Texas Gardener's Bible
Aggie horticulture (Texas A&M)   http://aggie-horticulture
.tamu.edu/

Plant Searches
Searches, plant lists, images   http://www.floridata.com/
Searches, images   http://hortiplex.gardenweb.com/plants/
Plant database   http://www.plantcare.com/
Dave's garden is huge.   http://davesgarden.com/

General Gardening Information
The old farmer's almanac   http://www.almanac.com/
Everything about gardening   http://www.mygardenguide.com/
Blogs, forums, gardening Q&A   http://www.gardenweb.com/
Great name and information   http://www.yougrowgirl.com/
Organic gardening   http://www.organicgardening.com/
Roses   http://www.everyrose.com/
Beautiful gardens for inspiration   http://www.americangarden
museum.com/

TV site; click on gardening   http://www.hgtv.com/
Attractively presented information   http://www.gardenguides
    .com/
Very helpful   http://www.helpfulgardener.com/
For the ambience of the South Seas   http://www.tropical
    gardening.com/
Where to find a plant   http://www.hortworld.com/
Amazon rainforest   http://www.rain-tree.com/
Nationwide plant exchange   http://www.gardennut.com/
Antique flower bulbs   http://www.oldhousegardens.com/

Houston Area Gardening Information

Great magazine for Texas gardeners   http://www.texas
    gardener.com/
Magazine for organic gardeners in Texas   http://homegrown
    texas.com
The name says it all.   http://www.houstongardening.info/
Personable and informative   http://www.burger.com/
    garden.htm
Texas gardening   http://neilsperry.com/
Growing old roses in Houston   http://www.texasroserustlers
    .org/
Fresh produce in Texas   http://www.picktexas.com
Friendly information   http://www.hal-pc.org/~trobb/
    horticul.html
Christmas tree farms   http://texaschristmastrees.com/
    houston.html

Houston

All about Houston   http://www.houston-guide.com/
Hermann Park   http://www.hermannpark.org/
Memorial Park   http://www.memorialparkconservancy.org/
Museum of Fine Arts   http://www.mfah.org
Children's Museum   http://www.cmhouston.org/
Contemporary Arts Museum   http://www.camh.org/
Buffalo Soldiers National Museum   http://www.buffalosoldier
    museum.com/
Holocaust Museum in Houston   http://www.hmh.org/

Orange Show   http://www.orangeshow.org/

Performing arts in Houston   http://www.houstontheater
district.org/

Cynthia Woods Mitchell Pavilion   http://pavilion.woodlands
center.org/

Houston Livestock Show and Rodeo   http://www.hlsr.com/

George Ranch Historical Park   http://georgeranch.org/

Old Town Spring   http://www.oldtownspringtx.com/

South of Houston

Space Center Houston (NASA)   http://www.spacecenter.org/

Seabrook   http://www.seabrook-tx.com/

Kemah Boardwalk   http://www.kemahboardwalk.com/

Joe's Boardwalk Beast (boat ride)   http://www.boardwalk
beast.com/

Galveston

Visitors Bureau   http://www.galveston.com/visitorinformation/

Galveston Island State Park
http://www.tpwd.state.tx.us/spdest/findadest/parks/galveston/

Schlitterbahn at Galveston Island Waterpark   http://www
.schlitterbahn.com/gal/

Grand 1894 Opera House   http://www.thegrand.com/

Tall ship *Elissa*   http://www.tsm-elissa.org/

Mardi Gras in Galveston   http://www.mardigrasgalveston.com/

Dickens on the Strand   http://www.dickensonthestrand.org/
events_overview.asp

North and West of Houston

All about Brenham and Round Top area   http://www
.brenhamtexas.com/

Bluebell Ice Cream   http://www.bluebell.com/

Festival Hill concerts and gardens   http://festivalhill.org/

Lady Bird Johnson Wildflower Center in Austin
http://www.wildflower.org/

Round Top Antiques Fair   http://roundtopantiquesfair.com/

Shakespeare at Winedale   http://www.shakespeare-winedale
.org/

Washington-on-the-Brazos   http://birthplaceoftexas.com/
Stay at a ranch   http://texasranchlife.com/
Bed and breakfast inns   http://www.bbonline.com/tx/

Potpourri

Gardening jokes and quotes   http://www.gardendigest.com/
humor.htm
Goldmine of computer tips, games, and more   http://www
.komando.com/
Courses for fun or profit   http://www.llu.com/
How far did you run?   http://www.gmap-pedometer.com/
Wine events in Houston   http://www.localwineevents
.com/Houston-Wine
Negotiating phone menus   http://gethuman.com/tips.html
Best seat on the plane   http://www.seatguru.com/
Cost of gas on a trip   http://www.fuelcostcalculator.com/
Geek on call 24/7   http://www.okteachme.com/index.html

Index

187

Index

ISBN-13: 978-1-58544-613-1
ISBN-10: 1-58544-613-0